Come Blow Your Horn

D1781252

A COMEDY IN THREE ACTS

By Neil Simon

SAMUEL FRENCH, INC.

45 WEST 25TH STREET   NEW YORK 10010

8   7623 SUNSET BOULEVARD   HOLLYWOOD 90046

LONDON   *TORONTO*

Printed in U.S.A.

ISBN 0 573 60713 3

Premiere Performance, February 22, 1961

Brooks Atkinson Theatre

William Hammerstein & Michael Ellis

present

"COME BLOW YOUR HORN"

A Comedy by

NEIL SIMON

CAST

(In Order of Appearance)

ALAN BAKER	*Hal March*
PEGGY EVANS	*Arlene Golonka*
BUDDY BAKER	*Warren Berlinger*
MR. BAKER	*Lou Jacobi*
CONNIE DAYTON	*Sarah Marshall*
MRS. BAKER	*Pert Kelton*
Λ VISITOR	*Carolyn Brenner*

Directed By Stanley Prager.

Settings and lights by Ralph Alswang.

Costumes by Stanley Simmons.

TIME: *The present.*

PLACE: *Alan's bachelor apartment in the East 60's, New York City.*

ACT I: *Six o'clock in the evening, early fall.*

ACT II: *Immediately after.*

ACT III: *Late afternoon. Three weeks later.*

Come Blow Your Horn

ACT ONE

SCENE: *The setting is the bachelor apartment of* ALAN
BAKER. *It is a very modern apartment consisting of a
living room, raised foyer, bedroom, bath (not seen)
and kitchen.* U. C. *is the modern flush door leading
from the hallway into the foyer. Just* L. *of the door is
a narrow guest closet door, practical. At the* L. *side
of the foyer is the door leading into the bedroom,
most of which is not seen.* L. *of the foyer, two steps
down into the living room, is a wall with a built-in
counter, desk and cabinet area to the* U. L. *corner.
This joins the* L. *wall running* D. L., *which also has
a bar area* U. L. *and counter cabinet extending* D. L.
In the U. L. *corner wall are three book or knicknack
shelves* L. *and* R. *of the corner.* C. *of* L. *wall is a large
picture casement window overlooking the Queens-
borough Bridge (backing).* R. *of the foyer (two steps
down) is a slate shelf running the entire length of
the* R. *rear wall,* C. *of which is a modern bronze fireplace chimney.* R. *and* L. *on foyer are short hand-
rails.* D. R. *of the fireplace is the entrance to the
kitchen, which includes a hanging accordion-pleated
door to separate this area from the living room. Ex-
treme* D. R. *is a counter such as a breakfast counter.
Modern blades run from counter to ceiling. The
foyer ceiling is lower than the living room ceiling with
a header running diagonally across the set.* D. R. C.
*is a modern upholstered chair with arms. Flanking
the fireplace are two matching upholstered chairs
without arms.* D. L. C. *is a curved upholstered modern
sofa, with a curved wooden table behind it. Below
the sofa is an oblong square coffee table.* U. L. *is a
desk kneehole chair. A modern hanging fixture lights*

5

the foyer. On the extended D. L. *counter is a modern lamp. Next to the* D. R. *counter is a modern bar stool. Various bric-a-brac and dressing is described in the prop list. There are five cover ceiling lights in the header in the* U. L. *corner shining down on the counters. The floor is carpeted wall to wall, including the foyer, with a dull gold rug.*

AT RISE: ALAN BAKER, *in a short Italian suede ski jacket, is standing in the doorway being his charming, persuasive best in attempting to lure* PEGGY EVANS, *pulling her into his bachelor apartment.* PEGGY *is in a ski outfit that fits her so snugly it leaves little room for skiing.* ALAN *puts down his valise (*L. *in foyer), then slides* PEGGY'S *overnight bag out of her hand without her even noticing it and places it on the floor.* ALAN *is very adept at this game. Being good-looking, bright, thirty-three and single, against* PEGGY'S *twenty-two years of blissful ignorance and eagerness to please, it appears that* ALAN *has all the marbles stacked on his side.*

PEGGY. Alan, no!
ALAN. Come on, honey.
PEGGY. Alan, no.
ALAN. (*Taking off her ski jacket. Puts on luggage.*) Just five more minutes. Come on.
PEGGY. Alan, no. Please. (*He pulls her into the living room. He* R. *of her*—D. C.)
ALAN. But you said you were cold.
PEGGY. I am.
ALAN. (*Embracing her.*) I'll start a fire. I'll have your blood going up and down in no time.
PEGGY. Alan, I want to go upstairs and take a bath. I've got about an inch of the New York Thruway on me.
ALAN. Honey, you can't go yet. We've got to have one last drink. To cap the perfect week end.
PEGGY. It was four days.
ALAN. It's not polite to count— Don't you ever get tired of looking sensational?
PEGGY. Do you think I do?

6

ALAN. You just saw what happened at the ski jump. They were looking at you and jumping into the parking lot— Come here. (*He bites her on the neck.*)

PEGGY. (*Giggles.*) Why do you always do that?

ALAN. Do what?

PEGGY. Bite me on the neck.

ALAN. What's the matter? You don't think I'm a vampire, do you?

PEGGY. Gee, I never thought of that.

ALAN. If it'll make you feel safer, I'll chew on your ear lobe. (*He does.*)

PEGGY. (*Giggles.*) Kiss me.

ALAN. I'm not through with the hors d'oeuvres yet. (*Nibbles—then he kisses her.*)

PEGGY. (*Sighs and sits on sofa.*) Now I feel warm again.

ALAN. Good.

PEGGY. Thank you for the week end, Alan. I had a wonderful time.

ALAN. Yeah, it was fun. (*Crossing* U. L. *toward bar.*)

PEGGY. Even though he didn't show up.

ALAN. (*Stops and turns.*) Who?

PEGGY. Your friend from M.G.M.

ALAN. (*Continuing to bar. Quickly.*) Oh, Mr. Manheim. Yeah— Well, that's show biz.

PEGGY. Did it say when he expects to be in New York again?

ALAN. Did what? (*Picks up carton containing Scotch bottle.*)

PEGGY. The telegram. From Hollywood.

ALAN. (*Crosses* D. L. *by window.*) Oh! Didn't I tell you? Next week. Early part.

PEGGY. It's kind of funny now that you think of it, isn't it?

ALAN. What is?

PEGGY. Him wanting to meet me in a hotel.

ALAN. (*Taking bottle out of carton.*) It was a ski lodge.

PEGGY. Was it? Anyway, it was nice. I've never been to New Hampshire before.

ALAN. It was Vermont. (*Putting down carton on sideboard.*)

PEGGY. Oh. I'm terrible with names. I can't imagine

why an important man like that wants to travel all the way up there just to meet me.

ALAN. (*Puts bottle back on bar. Crossing above R. and to R. of sofa.*) I explained all that. Since this picture he's planning is all about a winter carnival, he figured the best place to meet you would be against the natural setting of the picture. To see how you photograph against the snow. That makes sense— (*Not too sure.*) Doesn't it? (*Crosses R.*)

PEGGY. Oh, sure.

ALAN. Sure. (*Pulls PEGGY up from couch and embraces her.*)

PEGGY. We ought to go again sometime when it's not for business. Just for fun.

ALAN. *That* should be a week end.

PEGGY. Maybe next time I could learn to ski.

ALAN. I wouldn't be surprised.

PEGGY. It's a shame we were cooped up in the room so long.

ALAN. Yes. Well, I explained, we had that bad break in the weather.

PEGGY. You mean all that snow.

ALAN. Exactly— But you make the cutest little Saint Bernard— (*He is just about to kiss her when the BUZZER rings.*)

PEGGY. That's the lobby.

ALAN. I don't hear a thing.

PEGGY. Maybe it's for me.

ALAN. *My* buzzer? You live up in the penthouse.

PEGGY. I know. But I'm always here. (*He looks at her quizzically, then crossing U. L. C., goes to wall phone and picks it up. PEGGY turns U. R. C., fixing hair.*)

ALAN. (*Into phone.*) Yes?— Who?— Buddy?— Hi, kid— Now?— (*Looks at PEGGY.*) Well, sure. Sure, if it's important. You know the apartment. (*He hangs up.*) My kid brother. (*Crosses R. to her.*)

PEGGY. Oh. I'd better go.

ALAN. (*He reaches for her again.*) This is the seventh floor. We still have over a minute.

PEGGY. (*Eluding him, crosses Upstage to foyer. He follows. At R. rail.*) I want to go up and change, anyway.

8

(*She picks up her parka and goes* R. *to him, then says invitingly.*) You think he'll be here long?

ALAN. Not when you ask me like that.

PEGGY. Why don't you come up in twenty minutes?

ALAN. Why don't you come down in nineteen?

PEGGY. All right. 'Bye, Alan.

ALAN. (*Starts to embrace her.*) 'Bye, Connie.

PEGGY. Peggy! (*She breaks from him.*)

ALAN. What?

PEGGY. Peggy! That's the third time this week end you called me Connie.

ALAN. I didn't say Connie. I said, Honey!

PEGGY. Oh!

ALAN. Oh!

PEGGY. Sorry.

(ALAN *opens door. She smiles and exits. He closes door. ALAN breathes a sigh of relief. Picks up suitcase and goes into bedroom* U. L. *as the DOORBELL rings.*)

ALAN. (*Offstage.*) Come on in, it's open.

(BUDDY BAKER, *his younger brother, enters with a valise in hand. BUDDY is the complete opposite of ALAN. Reserved, unsure, shy.*)

BUDDY. Hello, Alan— Are you busy? (*Enters apartment and looks around—crosses* D. R. *to* L. *of* D. R. C. *chair.*)

ALAN. (*Offstage.*) No, no. Come in, kid. (*He re-enters.*) What's up? (*Crossing to* L. *of* BUDDY, ALAN *sees suitcase.*) What's in there?

BUDDY. Pajamas, toothbrush, the works. (*Puts suitcase down next to chair.*)

ALAN. You're kidding?

BUDDY. Nope.

ALAN. You mean you left? (BUDDY *nods.*) Permanently?

BUDDY. I took eight pairs of socks. For me that's permanently.

9

ALAN. I don't believe it. You can't tell me you actuallv ran away from home.

BUDDY. Well, I cheated a little. I took a taxi. (*Takes off coat and places it on suitcase.*)

ALAN. You're serious. You mean my baby brother finally broke out of prison?

BUDDY. We planned it long enough, didn't we?

ALAN. Yes, but every time I brought it up you said you weren't ready. Why didn't you say something to me?

BUDDY. When? You weren't at work since Thursday.

ALAN. Hey, did Dad say anything? About my being gone?

BUDDY. Not at the office. But at home he's been slamming doors. The chandelier in the foyer fell down. Where were you?

ALAN. (*Crosses L. above coffee table.*) Vermont.

BUDDY. Skiing?

ALAN. Only during the day. (*Sits on sofa and lights cigarette.*)

BUDDY. (*Crosses L. to sofa; one knee on arm.*) I don't know how you do it. If I'm at work one minute after nine, he docks my pay—and I get less to eat at home.

ALAN. Because he expects it from you. From me he says he expects nothing, so that's what I give him.

BUDDY. You're better off. At least you're not treated like a baby. You can talk with him.

ALAN. We don't talk. We have heart to heart threatening—

BUDDY. That's better than the subtle treatment I get. Last night I came home three o'clock in the morning. He didn't approve. What do you think he did? (ALAN *shakes his head.*) As I passed his bedroom door, he crc ved like a rooster. Cockle-doodle-doo.

ALAN. You're kidding? What'd you say?

BUDDY. Nothing. I wanted to cluck back like a r' icken but I didn't have the nerve.

ALAN. Oh, he's beautiful.

BUDDY. And then yesterday was my birthday. (*Sits on sofa R. of ALAN.*) Twenty-one years old.

ALAN. Oh, that's right. Gee. I'm sorry I wasn't there,

Buddy. Happy birthday, kid. (*He shakes* BUDDY's *hand warmly.*)

BUDDY. Thanks.

ALAN. I even forgot to get you a present.

BUDDY. I got one. A beaut. From Mom and Dad.

ALAN. What was it?

BUDDY. A surprise party. Mom, Dad and the Klingers.

ALAN. Who are the Klingers?

BUDDY. Oh, the Klingers are that lovely couple the folks met last summer at Lake Mahopac.

ALAN. Why? They're not your friends.

BUDDY. Think. Why would they have the Klingers there to meet me?

ALAN. They've got a daughter.

BUDDY. Oh, have they got a daughter.

ALAN. You mean they brought her with them?

BUDDY. In a crate.

ALAN. Let me guess. Naomi?

BUDDY. Close, Renee.

ALAN. Not much on looks but brilliant.

BUDDY. A genius. An I.Q. of 170. Same as her weight.

ALAN. And of course they had her dressed for the kill. They figured what she couldn't do, maybe Bergdorf could.

BUDDY. Nothing could help. So I spent the night of my twenty-first birthday watching a girl devour an entire bowl of cashew nuts.

ALAN. Oh, I'm sorry, kid.

BUDDY. (*Rises, crosses* R. C. *to chair.*) It's been getting worse and worse. He looks in my closets, my drawers. He listens to my phone calls. I don't know what it is I've done, Alan, but I swear he's going to turn me in. (*Sits* L. *arm of chair.*)

ALAN. (*Puts out cigarette.*) Well, it's simple enough. He's afraid you're going to follow in my footsteps.

BUDDY. I did. I thought it over all day and realized I had to leave. Well—here I am.

ALAN. Oh, I'm so proud of you, Buddy. If you weren't twenty-one, I'd kiss you.

BUDDY. (*Worried.*) You really think I did the right thing?

ALAN. What did you do, rob a bank? You're only going

11

to be living four subway stations away. You're still working for him, *aren't you?*

BUDDY. Well, there's going to be trouble there, too.

ALAN. What do you mean?

BUDDY. I know I'm going to be struck by lightning for saying this—but I'm thinking of leaving the business.

ALAN. On the level?

BUDDY. I'm not happy there, Alan. I'm not like you. You're good in the business—I'm not.

ALAN. It's just that you're inexperienced.

BUDDY. It's not only that. It just doesn't interest me. Gee whiz, there's a million more important things going on in the world today. New countries are being born. They're getting ready to send men to the moon. I just can't get excited about making wax fruit.

ALAN. Why not? It's a business like anything else.

BUDDY. It's different for you, Alan. You're hardly ever there. (*He sits chair* D. R. C.) You're the salesman, you're outside all day. Meeting people. Human beings. But I'm inside looking at petrified apples and pears and plums. They never rot, they never turn brown, they never grow old— It's like the fruit version of "The Picture of Dorian Gray."

ALAN. (*Follows.*) You know why you feel that way? Because you never get a chance to take the chains off. During the day it's all right. But at night you've got to bite into the *real* fruit of life, Buddy, not wax.

BUDDY. Yeah, I guess so.

ALAN. But that's all behind you now, right?

BUDDY. (*Crosses* D. L.) Well— (*He looks at his watch.*) In a few minutes anyway.

ALAN. (*Crosses* D. L.) What do you mean?

BUDDY. Dad should be coming home soon.

ALAN. (*Crosses* R. *to* BUDDY.) You mean you didn't tell him you were leaving?

BUDDY. I couldn't, Alan.

ALAN. Why not? Were you scared?

BUDDY. You bet I was. With you out of work these last few days he hasn't been all smiles. And besides—I just didn't want to hurt him. Sure he's stubborn and old-fashioned—but he means well.

ALAN. I know, kid. I understand.

BUDDY. I left him at the plant and came home early tonight. Then I wrote him a long letter explaining how I felt and left it on his bed. And in the morning, I think I'll be able to reason with him. Don't you?

ALAN. Frankly, no, but what's the difference? I'm proud of you. You walked out of Egypt, kid. How about a drink? To celebrate. (*He crosses to bar.*)

BUDDY. (*Sits on sofa.*) Sure—

ALAN. Scotch, Bourbon?

BUDDY. Scotch.

ALAN. Scotch it is.

BUDDY. And ginger ale.

ALAN. (*Stops.*) Scotch and-ginger ale?— They must know you in every bar in town. (*He makes drinks.*) Hey, how did Mom take all this?

BUDDY. (*Crosses and sits sofa, R. end.*) Oh, she's upset, of course. The most important thing to her is peace in the family.

ALAN. *And* a clean apartment.

BUDDY. (*Smiles.*) And a clean apartment.

ALAN. By the way, how is the Museum of Expensive Furniture?

BUDDY. Oh, the living room is still closed to the public!

ALAN. (*Crossing D. L. of sofa.*) Living room? I don't remember ever seeing a living room.

BUDDY. Sure you did. The one that had the lamp shades wrapped in cellophane for the past twenty years.

ALAN. (*Placing the drinks on coffee table.*) Oh, yes. I was outlawed from that room years ago for putting a cigarette in an ash tray. (*Sits L. of BUDDY.*)

BUDDY. But you know why I really left home? I don't wan't to have milk and cake standing over the sink any more. I want to sit in a chair and eat like real people.

ALAN. Whoa, boy. You've got to start easy, otherwise you'll get the bends. Maybe tonight you can hang your coat on the doorknob. Then maybe in a few days you'll be ready for bigger things—like leaving your socks on the floor.

BUDDY. (*Rises and swings around R. of C.*) Oh, it's going to be wonderful, just the two of us, Alan. (*He looks*

13

around.) Hey, I never realized it before, but this is a great apartment.

ALAN. Yeah. It comes a little high, but you pay for the atmosphere.

BUDDY. Oh, I almost forgot. How much is my rent?

ALAN. What rent?

BUDDY. For my share? I won't stay here unless I can pay my share.

ALAN. All right, sport. Give me thirty dollars.

BUDDY. Who are you kidding? This place is no sixty dollars a month.

ALAN. Look, that's your rent. Thirty dollars. When the old man starts paying you more, you can pay *me* more.

BUDDY. Well, just to start with. But we split everything else. The food and gas and electricity and everything. Agreed?

ALAN. (*Crosses* R. *to* BUDDY, *bringing a drink.*) Agreed. (*Hands* BUDDY *drink.*) Here. You owe me seventy-five cents. (*Raising his glass.*) Well, here's to the Baker Brothers. The dream we've planned for years. You take all the girls on the West Side, I'll take the East Side— and I'll get in trouble afore ye. (*He winks affectionately at* BUDDY. BUDDY *drinks,* ALAN *watches.*) How is it?

BUDDY (*Not very happy.*) Different.

ALAN. It should be. You just invented it. (*The PHONE rings.*) Ten to one it's a gorgeous girl. (*PHONE rings again. He picks up phone.*) Hello?— Oh, Mom!— How are you, gorgeous?— We were just talking about you— Yes, about ten minutes ago— He's fine— Of course I'm going to take care of him— All right, sweetheart. (*He holds phone out to* BUDDY.) It's the Curator of the Museum.

BUDDY. (*Crosses* L. *He takes the phone anxiously and sits sofa.* ALAN *crosses* R. *and above sofa and goes to bar for refill.*) Hello, Mom?— How are you?— Fine— Fine— No, no. I'll have dinner soon— I don't know, some place in the neighborhood— Mom— Did Dad read the letter yet?— Oh, still at the plant. (ALAN *crosses* D. L. *of sofa.* BUDDY *breathes a little easier.*) What?— Mom, I don't want you to hide the letter— I *want* him to read it— He what?— Oh, boy!

14

ALAN. What's wrong?

BUDDY. Well, I know that just makes it worse, Mom, but I can't— Mom!— Mom!— Mom!—

ALAN. She's crying?

BUDDY. (*Nods.*) She's crying.

ALAN. Crying.

BUDDY. (*Back into phone.*) Mom, please calm down— No, Mom, that's not fair of you to ask me that.

ALAN. What does she want you to do, come home?

BUDDY. (*Jumping up.*) Mom, don't tear up the letter. I can't come home.

ALAN. (*Crossing* D. R. *in front of table.*) Let me talk to her.

BUDDY. Mom, please-don't-tear-up-the-letter!

ALAN. (*Reaching for the phone.*) Give me the phone.

BUDDY. (*Turns away.*) Alan, will you wait a minute. (*Back into phone.*) All right, Mom. Let me think about it. I will. I'll call you back— Later— I promise— All right— Don't tear up the letter— Good-bye. (*He hangs up.*)

ALAN. You'll think about what?

BUDDY. Dad called Mom about ten minutes ago from the plant. Screaming. Some customer is angry at you! Because you didn't show up for a meeting today?

ALAN. (*Turns front.*) Oh, my gosh, Mr. Meltzer; I forgot.

BUDDY. Anyway, Mom's afraid when she finds out that I left on top of this he'll go to pieces.

ALAN. All right, all right. One thing has nothing to do with the other. I'll straighten him out.

BUDDY. But he's going to let this all out on Mom. And you know him when he starts to yell. You could get killed just from the fallout.

ALAN. Well, what do you want to do?

BUDDY. I don't know. Maybe I should go home. (*Picks up coat and suitcase.*)

ALAN. Go home? Why?

BUDDY. Why should Mom get the blame for something we've done?

ALAN. (*Follows to* L. *of* BUDDY.) Don't ask me. I don't crow like a rooster at three o'clock in the morning.

BUDDY. What am I supposed to do?

ALAN. Grow up. Be a man. You're twenty-one years old. (*Takes his suitcase and coat and puts them down by* U. R. *end of sofa.*)

BUDDY. You mean just forget about it?

ALAN. (*Crosses to him.*) Buddy, how long do you want to wait until you start enjoying life? When you're sixty-five you get social security, not girls.

BUDDY. I don't know how we got all twisted around. I'm on your side. I want to leave. It's Dad who's against it.

ALAN. Buddy, I know he means well. But he'll just never understand that things in life change. He's been in the waxed fruit business too long. *You've* changed.

BUDDY. I know, but—

ALAN. You're twenty-one years old now. You're ripe. Come on, kid. You've got one shoe off. Kick the other one off.

BUDDY. (*Looks at* ALAN *a moment, then shrugs.*) I—I guess you're right.

ALAN. Then you'll stay?

BUDDY. (*Nods.*) Yeah— Why not?

ALAN. (*Puts arm around him.*) That's the kid brother I love and adore. Now go put your stuff in the bedroom.

BUDDY. You sure I won't be in your way here or anything? (*Picking up his coat and suitcase, starts Upstage.*)

ALAN. Of course not. We just may have to work out a traffic system. I've got a girl coming down in a few minutes.

BUDDY. A girl? Why didn't you say so? Whenever you want to be alone, just say the word. I'll go out to a movie.

ALAN. Don't worry. With my schedule, you won't miss a picture this year. (*The DOORBELL rings.*) You hear that? She's here ten minutes ahead of time. (*The DOOR-BELL rings again.*) Coming! (*Swings up on foyer to door.*)

BUDDY. I'd better put this in here and go. (*Goes into bedroom* U. L.)

ALAN. No, no. I want you to see her first. (*He crosses to door.*) Ready for the thrill of your life? (*He opens the door a crack as he says:*) and my third wish, O Geni, is that when I open the door, the most beautiful girl in the

16

world will be standing there. (*He motions* BUDDY *to come out of bedroom. As he opens the door, there stands his* FATHER, *scowling disgustedly*.) Dad!! (BUDDY *enters and immediately goes back into bedroom closing door quietly behind him.* FATHER *steps in and looks at* ALAN *and nods disgustedly. He walks into the room* D. R. *of* D. R. C. *chair and* L. *below it.* ALAN *looks after him dismayed, and seems puzzled when he doesn't see* BUDDY. *The* FATHER *examines the room. It is obvious he approves of nothing in the apartment. Meeting him* D. C.) Gee, Dad—this is a—pleasant—surprise. (*The* FATHER *looks at him as if to say* "I'll bet.") How—how are you?

FATHER. How am I?— I'll tell you sometime.— That's how I am. (*He continues his inspection. Crosses* L. *of* ALAN *to coffee table.*)

ALAN. I've redecorated the place— How do you like it?

FATHER. Fancy— Very fancy— You must have some nice job. (*Sniffs highball glass.*)

ALAN. I just got in, Dad. I was about to call you.

FATHER. The phone company shouldn't have to depend on your business.

ALAN. I wanted to explain what happened to me. Why I wasn't in the last two days.

FATHER. (*Crosses* R. *a step.*) There's nothing to explain.

ALAN. Yes, there is, Dad.

FATHER. Why? I understand. You work very hard two days a week and you need a five-day week end. That's normal.

ALAN. Dad, I'm not going to lie. I was up in Vermont skiing. I intended to be back Sunday night, but I twisted my bad ankle again. I couldn't drive. I thought it was broken.

FATHER. I'll send you a get-well card.

ALAN. I'm sorry, Dad. I really am.

FATHER. You're sorry. I can't ask more than that.

ALAN. I'll be in the office first thing in the morning.

FATHER. That's good news. You know the address, don't you?

ALAN. Yes, Dad. I know the address.

FATHER. See. I always said you were smart. So I'll see you in the morning.

ALAN. Right! (*He starts Upstage.*)

FATHER. (*Doesn't move.*) Oh, by the way— How's the Meltzer account going?

ALAN. The Meltzer account? (*He comes back R. of him.*)

FATHER. From Atlantic City? The one you bragged about was all wrapped up?

ALAN. Oh—er—fine.

FATHER. Fine? I'm glad to hear that— Because he called today.

ALAN. (*Surprised.*) Oh? About an order?

FATHER. Yes. About an order.

ALAN. (*A little skeptical.*) Did—did we get one?

FATHER. Yes— We got one.

ALAN. How much?

FATHER. How much? Guess.

ALAN. Well, Dad, I—

FATHER. Guess! Guess how much we got from Meltzer.

ALAN. Nothing?

FATHER. Bingo! Right on the button! Bum! (*Points to him sharply.*)

ALAN. Dad, wait a minute—

FATHER. (*Crossing to him. Each "Bum" is a sharp point.*) Did you have a nice week end, bum? Do you know what it costs to go skiing for four days? Three thousand dollars a day? Bum!

ALAN. I tried to call him. I couldn't get a line through.

FATHER. On skis you tried to call him? You should be in the Olympics.

ALAN. (*Crossing L. to phone.*) I'll call him right back. I'll explain everything. (*Sits sofa and picks up phone.*)

FATHER. (*Turns.*) Where you gonna call him?

ALAN. In Atlantic City.

FATHER. Who're you going to talk to? The Boardwalk? He's here!

ALAN. In New York?

FATHER. In the Hotel Croyden. For two days he's sitting waiting while you're playing in the snow. (*Imitates playing, a step D. R.*)

ALAN. (*Hangs up phone, crosses R. to* FATHER.) Dad, I promise you. I won't lose the account!

FATHER. Why? This would be the first one you ever lost? You want to see the list? You could *ski*— (*Gestures.*) down your cancellations.

ALAN. I couldn't get back in time, Dad. Skiing had nothing to do with it.

FATHER. (*Crossing* D. L. *to sofa.*) I'm sorry. I forgot. I left out golf and sailing and sleeping and drinking and women. You're terrific. (*Turns to him.*) If I was in the bum business I would want ten like you.

ALAN. (*Step* L. *to* C.) That's not true. I put in plenty of time in the business.

FATHER. (*A step* R.) Two years. In six years you put in two years. I had my bookkeeper figure it out.

ALAN. Thank you.

FATHER. (*Looks at him, turns.*) My own son. I get more help from my competitors. (*Starts to sit* R. *end sofa.*)

ALAN. Well, why not? You treat me like one.

FATHER. (*Jumping up, crosses* R. *to* C.) *I* treat you? Do *I* wander in eleven o'clock in the morning? Do *I* take three hours for lunch—in night clubs? When are you there? (*Crosses* R. *to him.*)

ALAN. What do you mean, when?

FATHER. (*Backs* L. *to* C.) When? When? You take off legal holidays, Jewish holidays, Catholic holidays. Last year you took off Hallowe'en.

ALAN. I was sick.

FATHER. (*Turns* R.) When you came back to work you were sick. When you were sick you were dancing. (*Turns* L., *imitating dancing.*)

ALAN. (*Crosses* L. *to him.*) In the first place, it's not true. And in the second place what good does it do coming in? You don't need me. You never ask my advice about the business, do you?

FATHER. What does a skier know about waxed fruit?

ALAN. (*Crosses away* R. C.) You see. You see. You won't even listen.

FATHER. (*He sits sofa,* R. *end.*) Come in early. I'll listen.

ALAN. (*Crosses* L. *to him.*) I did. For three years. Only then I was "too young" to have anything to say. And now that I've got my own apartment, I'm too much of a "bum"

19

to have anything to say. Admit it, Dad. You don't give me the same respect you give the night watchman.

FATHER. At least I know where he is at nights.

ALAN. You know where I am, too. Having fun. What's wrong with it? I think what I do at night should be my business.

FATHER. Not when it's nighttime four days in a row. Listen, what do I care. (*He rises and crosses* R. *of* ALAN *to* D. R. C. *chair.*) Do whatever you want. Go ahead and live like a bum.

ALAN. Why am I a bum?

FATHER. Are you married?

ALAN. No.

FATHER. Then you're a bum!

ALAN. Give me a chance. I'll get married.

FATHER. (*Crossing* L. *to him.*) I heard that for years. When you were 26, 27, 28, even 29, you were a bachelor. But now you're over thirty and you're still not married, so you're a bum and that's all there is to it. (*Turns away* R.)

ALAN. Who made thirty the closing date? All I want to do is have a little fun out of life like any other healthy, normal American boy.

FATHER. (*Turns to him.*) Healthy you are, American you are, normal you're not.

ALAN. What do you mean?

FATHER. Look at your brother, that's what I mean. That's normal. He'll be something, that kid. He'll never be like you. Not in a million years.

ALAN. (*Crosses* U. *to* R. *end of sofa and leans against back of sofa.*) Really? He might surprise you.

FATHER. (*Crosses* D. R.) That I'll bet my life on. He's in the plant the first thing in the morning, he puts in a whole day's work. No, that's one son I'll never have to worry about! (*Front.*)

ALAN. Have you read your mail lately?

FATHER. (*Turns.*) What?

ALAN. Nothing.

FATHER. (*Crosses* U. *to* R. *end of foyer steps, not on.*) All right, I don't want to discuss anything more. I want to see you in the office tomorrow morning at eight o'clock.

ALAN. (*Crosses* U. *to* L. *of him.*) Eight o'clock? There's no one there then.

FATHER. You'll be there. And you'll be there two nights a week and Saturdays, holidays, birthdays and vacations. I'm sick and tired of being the father. From now on I'm the boss.

ALAN. All right, Dad, but eight o'clock is silly. I have nothing to do until nine.

FATHER. You play solitaire all day, anyway. You can get in three more games. (*Crossing up to foyer.*)

ALAN. Okay. Okay, I'll be there.

FATHER. (*Turns and points.*) *With* the Meltzer account. If you haven't got it signed and in your pocket— you can ski— (*Gesturing.*) right into the unemployment office.

ALAN. (*Crosses* D. R. C.) I'll try, Dad. I'll really do my best.

FATHER. With your best, we're in trouble. From you I need a miracle. (ALAN *sits* D. R. C. *chair.*) Eight o'clock with the Meltzer account— (*Crosses to door.*)

ALAN. Yes, Dad.

FATHER. (*Turns.*) The day your brother becomes like you, I throw myself in front of an airplane. (*And with that he exits.*)

(*As front door slams,* BUDDY *comes rushing out of the bedroom door in a state of shock.*)

BUDDY. (*Crosses* R. *to* L. *of* ALAN.) Did you near that? I told you, Alan. I told you what he'd do.

ALAN. (*Crosses* L. *to phone. Sits.*) What hotel did he say, the Croyden?

BUDDY. (*Follows to* C.) Wait'll he reads that letter. He'll kill himself. He'll kill all of us. Like those stories in the Daily News. Alan, give me the phone.

ALAN. (*He dials* 411.) Take it easy, will you? I've got to call Meltzer.

BUDDY. (*Swings away* R.) Meltzer? We've got to get to Mom before he gets home. She's got to tear up that letter. (*Turns, crosses* L. *to* ALAN.)

ALAN. Will you relax. He's not going to kill anyone until he's had his supper— I'll straighten everything out.

BUDDY. How?

ALAN. All I've got to do is get Meltzer to sign. (*Into phone.*) I'd like the number of the Hotel Croyden, please.

BUDDY. Suppose you don't?

ALAN. There's no problem. He came to New York because I promised him a party— (*Into phone.*) What was that? Thank you. (*Dials number.*)

BUDDY. (*Crossing D. R.*) I sure picked a rotten time to leave. It's going to be murder up there. (*Starts to go U. C.*) I'm going home.

ALAN. (*Rises. Stops him with.*) You walk out that door, I don't want you back.

BUDDY. (*Coming back C.*) Alan, why don't you help me?

ALAN. (*Into phone.*) Mr. Martin Meltzer, please— Thank you. (*To BUDDY.*) I'm doing more than helping you. I'm saving you. It took you two years to get this far. Next time it'll take you five. (*Into phone and rises, crosses L. of coffee table.*) Hello? Mr. Meltzer? Hi? Alan Baker!— Where was I?— I'm too embarrassed to tell you— You ready?— Atlantic City— Yes. I thought you wanted me to come *there*— I just didn't think— Sure, I had the girls with me—

BUDDY. (D. R.) You're a lunatic!

ALAN. (*Covers phone quickly.*) Will you shut up? (*Back into phone.*) What?— Well, can't you take the morning train back?— Can I still get in touch with the girls? They're here with me right now.

BUDDY. (*Yells.*) Where?

ALAN. (*Covers phone again quickly.*) I'll shove you in the closet. (*Back into phone; BUDDY crosses U. R. of foyer steps.*) What was that?— Yes— That was one of the girls you heard— Pretty? (*He laughs. Turns head slightly from phone.*) Honey, he wants to know if you're pretty— Mr. Meltzer, did you ever see an ugly girl in the Copacabana line?— No, they're off this week— Yes, they're dying to— Your hotel. Room 326— Half hour? You have the drinks ready, I'll bring the drinkers. (*He laughs a phony laugh into the phone and hangs up.*) I hate myself.

(*He picks up book and thumbs through it quickly. Sits sofa.*)

BUDDY. I never saw anyone like you. Is it like this every night? (*Sits* R. *end foyer steps.*)

ALAN. Well, it's always slow before Christmas. (*Reading from book.*) "Married—Married—Europe—Pregnant —" (*Finds something in book.*) Ahhh, here we are. Chickie Parker. (*He dials.*)

BUDDY. Chickie Parker?

ALAN. And she looks just like she sounds. (*Into phone.*) Hello?— Chickie? Don't you know you could be arrested for having such a sexy voice?— Alan— (*Rises, steps* L.) How could I? I just got in from Europe an hour ago— Switzerland— A specialist there told me if I don't see you within a half an hour, I'll die— Yes, tonight— A friend of mine is having a little party— Wonderful guy— hundred laughs— Hey, Chickie, is your roommate free? The French girl?— Wonderful. Yes. Bring her— No, I can't. I've got to get the pretzels. Can you meet me there? The Hotel Croyden, Room 326, Marty Meltzer— A half hour— Marvelous. I just love you— What?— Yes, Alan Baker. (*He hangs up. Looks quizzically at phone.*) Viola!

BUDDY. (*He's flabbergasted.*) And it took me three months to get a date for my prom.

ALAN. I'd better get going. (*He starts for bedroom when the BUZZER rings. He stops.*) Now what? (*He crosses* L. *quickly to intercom phone and speaks into it.*) Hello?— Who? (*Big surprise.*) Connie!— What are you doing here?— No, honey, no— Now?— Well, sure—sure, come on. (*He hangs up.*) Of all the nights! (*Steps Downstage.*)

BUDDY. (*Rises, crosses* L. *to him.*) Who's that?

ALAN. A girl.

BUDDY. Another one? Is she coming up? (ALAN *nods.*)

ALAN. (*Half to himself, crosses* D. R. *of sofa.*) She wasn't due back in town till tomorrow. What a time to show up.

BUDDY. (*Follows* R. *of him.*) Then why are you seeing her?

ALAN. Oh, I can't give this girl the brush.

BUDDY. I thought that part would be easy.

ALAN. You don't understand. This girl is different. She's not like— (*Indicates phone and upstairs.*) well, she's different.

BUDDY. You mean this one's for serious?

ALAN. (*Crosses* D. L.) Who said serious? I just said different.

BUDDY. Oh boy, would that solve everything at home if you got married. Mom's had an open line to the caterers for three years now.

ALAN. (*Crosses* R. *of* C.) Married? Me? With all this? Are you crazy?

BUDDY. (*Turns* R.) Well, I just thought—since she's a *nice* girl—

ALAN. She's the *nicest*—but I'm working on it. Listen, you'd better blow. I want to see her alone.

(*DOORBELL rings.*)

BUDDY. Okay. (*He starts Upstage for the door.*)

ALAN. (*Stops him, shoos him* R. *to kitchen.*) Oh! Hey, go out the service entrance in the kitchen— I haven't got time for lengthy introductions. Come back in a few minutes.

BUDDY. (*He nods, turns at kitchen doorway* R.) Boy, no wonder you come in eleven o'clock in the morning! (*He exits* R.)

ALAN. (*He crosses quickly to the door and opens it about an inch and says aloud:*) And my third wish, O Geni, is that when I open my eyes, the most beautiful girl in the world will be standing there. (*He opens door, turns and looks.* CONNIE *is standing there, holding an octagonal hat box. Crossing* D. R. *to* D. R. C. *chair.*) O Joy! My third wish has been granted. Enter, beautiful lady. (CONNIE *enters. Puts purse on foyer table.*)

CONNIE. (*Crosses* D. *to* C.) Well, I guess it's safe as long as you've used up the other two wishes.

ALAN. (*Crosses* L. *to her.*) How are you, Connie?

CONNIE. Fine—now that I'm back.

ALAN. (*He embraces her.*) Mmm. How does a girl get to smell like that?

24

CONNIE. She washes occasionally. (*Holding package between them.*)

ALAN. Come here. I've been thinking about this moment for two whole weeks. (*He tries to get closer.*) Will you put down that package.

CONNIE. (*She presents it to him.*) After you open it.

ALAN. (*He takes it.*) What is it?

CONNIE. A present.

ALAN. For me? Why?

CONNIE. (*She shrugs.*) I like you! And I missed you.

ALAN. Well, I did too, but I didn't get you a present.

CONNIE. Well, don't get upset about it. I just like you six dollars and ninety-eight cents more than you like me. Open it. (*Unbottons jacket.*)

ALAN. (*He opens it and looks in box. He is overwhelmed.*) Connie! My ski hat! (*He takes it out of box.*)

CONNIE. It's like the one you lost, isn't it?

ALAN. (*He is really quite thrilled with it.*) It's the same thing. (*He looks inside at the label.*) It's the identical one I bought in Switzerland. I've looked all over New York for this. (*Puts box on L. fireplace chair.*) Where did you ever get it?

CONNIE. In Montreal— (*He puts hat on. She puts jacket on R. end of sofa.*)

ALAN. It even fits. How did you know my head size?

CONNIE. I've got an imprint on my neck.

ALAN. (*Throws hat on sofa.*) Connie, you're wonderful. Only *you* would think of a thing like this.

CONNIE. (*Turns to hat.*) Well, I *thought* of a watch, but I could afford this better.

ALAN. Come here, you. (*He takes her in his arms.*)

CONNIE. (*Coyly.*) Ah, the payoff.

ALAN. Thank you very much. (*He kisses her.*)

CONNIE. You're welcome—very much. (ALAN *moves to embrace her. She backs away* L.) Alan, relax.

ALAN. I'm not through thanking you yet.

CONNIE. (*She crosses* D. L. *of sofa.*) I've just come eight hundred miles in a prehistoric train and I'm tired, hungry and too weak to be chased around the sofa.

ALAN. (*Crosses* L. *to* CONNIE.) I'll carry you. We'll save lots of time and energy. (*He moves after her.*)

25

CONNIE. Alan, please don't take advantage. I've got enough handicaps as it is.

ALAN. Like what?

CONNIE. (*Wilting.*) Like being on your side. (*He grabs her and she swings down around* R. *of him.*) No, Alan! It isn't fair. You and me against me is not fair. What is it you've got?

ALAN. I don't know. Am I terribly good-looking?

CONNIE. Oh, God, no. You've got just enough things wrong with your face to make you very attractive. It's something else. Some strange power you have over me. (*He tries to kiss her. She breaks and crosses* R. *of* C.) But beware. The day I find out what it is, I'll have a gypsy destroy the spell with a dead chicken.

ALAN. You little fool. Nothing can stop the Phantom Lover. (*He starts after her.*)

CONNIE. Alan, no! (*Backs* R. *above* D. R. C. *chair.*)

ALAN. (*Stalking her* R., L. *of chair.*) One kiss. If it leaves you cold, I'll stop. But if it gets you all crazy, we play house rules.

CONNIE. (*Moves* R. *so chair* R. *is between them.*) Now, Alan, play fair.

ALAN. I'll keep my hands behind my back. I'll spot you a five-point lead, I'll only be permitted to use my upper lip. (*Steps up on chair.*)

CONNIE. Alan, not now. Please. I haven't got the strength to put up an interesting fight. I just wanted to see you before I fell into bed for the next week and a half.

ALAN. Okay. (*He pecks her.*) A rough tour, heh? (*He gets down off chair.*)

CONNIE. This was the roughest. (*Sits on* R. *arm of chair.*)

ALAN. (*He laughs, sits* D. R. C. *chair.*) You poor kid. When does the show go out again?

CONNIE. *They* leave in two weeks.

ALAN. They? Not you?

CONNIE. (*Smiles.*) Not me.

ALAN. Why not?

CONNIE. I just suddenly decided to quit.

ALAN. Oh. Well, have you got another show lined up?

CONNIE. Well—it's not just the show I quit. It's the show business.

ALAN. (*He looks at her.*) Are you serious?

CONNIE. (*She nods. She doesn't want to make a big thing of it now.*) I'll tell you all about it tomorrow. (*Starts* L.) Will you call me, darling? In the afternoon?

ALAN. (*Crosses* L. *to* C.) Wait a minute. I want to hear about this.

CONNIE. (*At* R. *end of sofa.*) There's nothing to tell.

ALAN. Nothing to tell? You're giving up your career and there's nothing to tell?

CONNIE. (*She laughs.*) Oh, Alan, darling—what career?

ALAN. What do you mean, what career? You're a singer, aren't you?

CONNIE. Well, I wouldn't invest in it.

ALAN. I don't get it. Things are going so well for you— All those musicals you do.

CONNIE. (*Sits sofa* C.) They're not musicals. They're industrial shows. Two-hour commercials completely uninterrupted by entertainment.

ALAN. (*Sits* R. *of her and puts hat on table behind sofa.*) I'm serious.

CONNIE. I'm dead serious. This past month we did a show for the Consolidated Meat Packers. Have you any idea what it's like singing "Why Not Take All of Me" dressed as a sausage?

ALAN. (*He smiles.*) It sounds funny.

CONNIE. Maybe to you. But I've seen butchers sit there and cry.

ALAN. All right, so it's not "My Fair Lady." You don't expect it to come easy, do you?

CONNIE. I don't expect it to come at all. Not now. Alan— (*Breaks* L.) I'd work my throat to the bone if I thought I had a chance—or if I wanted it that much. But somehow lately I don't care any more— I guess it started when I met you. (*Sits* L. *arm of sofa.*)

ALAN. Honey, everyone gets discouraged. But you don't suddenly throw away a promising career.

CONNIE. Promising? Even you once said I was a lousy singer.

27

ALAN. No, I didn't. I said you had a lousy voice. There's a big difference.

CONNIE. There is?

ALAN. Of course. You've got looks, personality. That's all you need in the music business today. Hockey players are making albums.

CONNIE. It's *not* enough, Alan. You've got to have talent, too.

ALAN. Only if you want to be good. Not if you want to be a star.

CONNIE. Well, it's pretty evident I'm not going to be either.

ALAN. I just don't understand your attitude.

CONNIE. (*Rises.*) I don't understand *yours*. The world isn't losing one of its great artists.

ALAN. What suddenly brought all this on?

CONNIE. (*Sits L. of him.*) It's very simple. I just got tired of being away from you so long.

ALAN. (*Withdrawing slightly — turns front.*) Oh! Well—if that's what you want.

CONNIE. That's it. No more travelling. No more buses and trains and long distance phone calls. (*She moves closer.*) I don't want to be more than a thirty-five-cent taxi ride away from you.

ALAN. (*Getting a little jittery.*) You—seem to have made up your mind.

CONNIE. Yes. And what a relief it is.

ALAN. (*Looks at her.*) Well—what will you do now?

CONNIE. (*Pauses, looks at him.*) I'll manage. (ALAN *rises, drifts R. of C.*) Girls are doing it every day. I'll maybe do a little modeling or become a secretary. Or—a housewife.

ALAN. (*Turns to face her.*) What?

CONNIE. Housewife. You know—sleep-in maids.

ALAN. (*Serious.*) What do you mean?

CONNIE. It was a joke—you didn't get it.

ALAN. (*Dead pan.*) Yeah, I get it. It's funny. (*Looks at his watch.*) Holy mackerel, look at the time. (*Starts U. L.*) Honey, I'm awfully sorry, but I've got an important business appointment. Can I call you later? (*Picks up her jacket.*)

CONNIE. No. I want to finish talking.

ALAN. About what?

CONNIE. Housewives.

ALAN. What about them?

CONNIE. You act as if you never heard of them.

ALAN. Sure I did. My mother's a housewife.

CONNIE. So's Elizabeth Taylor. Don't distort the picture.

ALAN. Connie, sweetheart— This is serious talk. Let's set aside a whole night for it. But right now I've really got to run. (*Holds her jacket out for her.*)

CONNIE. How far?

ALAN. What?

CONNIE. I must have touched a nerve or something.

ALAN. That's not true. We've discussed marriage before, haven't we?

CONNIE. Yes. On this very couch. Or were they just campaign promises?

ALAN. What difference did it make? I didn't win the election, did I?

CONNIE. The returns aren't all in yet.

ALAN. (*He looks at his watch nervously.*) Connie, honey. *You're* tired and I've got a business appointment—— (*Holds jacket out again.*)

CONNIE. At seven o'clock?

ALAN. It won't take long. I can be through by ten.

CONNIE. I'll bet you can.

ALAN. What do you mean?

CONNIE. Oh, Alan, I'm a big girl. You've got a date.

ALAN. It's a business appointment. And besides, 1 didn't expect you back until tomorrow.

CONNIE. You know, something just occurred to me. (*Rises.*) A few minutes ago I couldn't understand why you were fighting so hard to keep me in show business. It's suddenly very clear.

ALAN. What is?

CONNIE. It's not *my* career you're worried about. It's *yours!*

ALAN. *My* career?

CONNIE. As a lover. (*Grabs jacket and crosses* R. C., L.

of D. R. C. *chair.*) That's why you want me to stay out on the road.

ALAN. (*Crosses to* L. *of her.*) Why? I'm crazy about you.

CONNIE. Yes—when I'm here. The minute I leave—substitution. Oh, it's beautiful. A bachelor's dream. The two-platoon system. (*Putting on jacket.*)

ALAN. What are you talking about?

CONNIE. (*Buttoning jacket.*) You'll never grow stale, Alan. Or bored. Not as long as you keep rotating the crops every two weeks.

ALAN. That's not true.

CONNIE. I'll bet you've got a regular schedule. A timetable—with arrivals and departures. Love on a shuttle.

ALAN. You're not being fair. (*Crossing* D. L., R. *of sofa.*) I never said I didn't want to get married. But you come in here and make it sound like an emergency.

CONNIE. For some strange reason I thought you felt the same as I did. These past six months were—

ALAN. (*Crosses to her.*) They were wonderful. That's why I hate to see them end.

CONNIE. END! Getting married is the end?

ALAN. I didn't mean it that way. Connie, you've got to understand, in a way a thirty-three-year-old guy is a lot younger than a twenty-four-year-old girl. That is, he may not be ready for marriage yet.

CONNIE. Let's leave the third person out of this. You mean you.

ALAN. The point is, I didn't actually start my bachelor fling until late in life. And to tell the truth, I don't know if I'm flung out yet.

CONNIE. You would be if you were in love with me.

ALAN. I am. Very much in love—only—I don't know. I'm like a kid with a few chocolates left in the box. I want to finish them first.

CONNIE. Will you stop twisting thoughts? Now you're making it sound as if I'm taking candy from a baby. (*Crosses* R. *and sits* D. R. C. *chair.*)

ALAN. (*Crosses to* U. L. *of her.*) No, I'm not. I'm leveling with you. Sure I see other girls. I'm only human but— (*Crossing* L. *toward bar.*) you must admit although

30

these past six months were wonderful and exciting, I *have* made certain sacrifices that go against the very nature of man. (*Turns to her.*) And you know from whence I speak. (*Crosses to bar.*)

CONNIE. The subject hasn't exactly been taboo.

ALAN. (*Crosses D. L. of sofa.*) True, it was discussed. But it never got off the drawing board. If it were another girl, I'd be in Tahiti painting by now. But here I am. Still battling it out.

CONNIE. The war would be over if I knew just what it was we were fighting for.

ALAN. I don't think I follow that.

CONNIE. (*Moves to edge of chair.*) All right, then, Alan, let's have the truth. Either you've said to yourself "I'm going to marry this girl," or "I'm going to have an affair with her." All I ask is that you let me in on your decision. If marriage is out just say so. I won't run. I'll stay and fight for my honor the way a girl who's been properly brought up should. And I can truthfully tell you I'll lose the battle before long, because, damn it, I'm in love with you. But if you're really in love with me, you've got to tell me and be prepared to back it up with the rest of your life. (*Rises.*) Well, which is it going to be, Alan? Do we march down the aisle or into the bedroom?

ALAN. (*He stares at her unbelievingly a few seconds.*) That's the lousiest thing I ever heard. What am I supposed to say? (*Starts R.*)

CONNIE. Say what you really feel.

ALAN. (*To her L.*) You mean if I want to make love to you all I have to do is speak up?

CONNIE. Loud and clear.

ALAN. You're a nut. (*Breaks L.*) A sweet, beautiful nut!

CONNIE. I'm waiting, Alan.

ALAN. (*Turning to her.*) For what? If I say I want you, you're mine. If I say I love you, I'm yours.

CONNIE. It's that simple.

ALAN. Well, I'm not going to play. (*Crosses L. of coffee table.*) It's more dangerous than Russian Roulette.

CONNIE. It's just being honest with each other, Alan.

That's what you're afraid of. You won't even be honest with yourself.

ALAN. How can I be? I don't know what I want yet.

CONNIE. I didn't say you *had* to love me. I just want to know if you do.

ALAN. (*Crossing* R. *to* C.) If I want you I don't have to love you, but if I love you I shouldn't want you—I—I don't know. You've got to be an I.B.M. machine to figure out this affair. (*Turns to* U. R. *corner of sofa.*)

CONNIE. I guess so. I forgot to make room for human failing.

ALAN. Boy, oh boy, for an innocent little girl you sure play rough.

CONNIE. I didn't choose the game, Alan. (*She starts Upstage to go.*)

ALAN. Where are you going? (*He stops her.*)

CONNIE. (*Turns. At bottom step,* R. *end.*) I'd say you needed a chance to think.

ALAN. No, I don't.

CONNIE. You mean you've made up your mind?

ALAN. Yes— Yes, I've made up my mind.

CONNIE. Well?

ALAN. You mean, no matter what I say, you'll go along with it?

CONNIE. To the letter.

ALAN. Okay— Okay, then. We march into the bedroom.

CONNIE. (*Stares at him.*) That's the lousiest thing I ever heard.

ALAN. (*Sits* R. *arm of sofa.*) Uh-huh. You see? You see? It's not so much fun when the *dentist* is sitting in the chair is it? You don't like it when I hold the drill.

CONNIE. I'm not complaining, Alan. I asked for it.

ALAN. Oh, that you did. And I called your little bluff, didn't I?

CONNIE. You certainly did. (*She goes up to door, gets purse.*)

ALAN. Where are you going?

CONNIE. Back to my hotel.

ALAN. (*Crossing up* L. *of her.*) All right, wait a second, Connie. The joke is over. You're embarrassed because I made you lose face. I'm sorry. But when you pushed me into a corner like that I had no choice.

CONNIE. Oh, my face is still all there, Alan. I just figure if I'm going into business here I might as well get the rest of my merchandise. (*She goes blowing him a kiss. Closes door.* ALAN *stares after her.*)

ALAN. No— Never happen— (*Crosses* D. *to* R. *end of sofa.*) Not her— (*The DOORBELL rings.* ALAN *rushes to it. He opens it expectantly; it's* BUDDY.) Oh, it's you.

BUDDY. Hey, was that her?

ALAN. (*Reaches in closet for trench coat.*) Where'd you go?

BUDDY. Downstairs for a sandwich. Now, that's what I call a pretty girl.

ALAN. (*He gets coat from closet.*) You stay away from that kind. They're nothing but trouble. (*Starts putting on coat.*)

BUDDY. How did it go?

ALAN. Oh, fine. Fine.

BUDDY. I thought maybe the other girl walked in.

ALAN. What other girl?

BUDDY. The one you were expecting. From upstairs. Didn't you call her?

ALAN. Peggy! Oh, my gosh, I forgot. (*He crosses quickly to telephone. Sits, throwing coat over sofa-back.*)

BUDDY. (*Crosses* D. R. *to* C.) You ought to get one of those maps with the stick pins so you know where they are all the time.

ALAN. (*Dialing.*) I don't know what I'm doing tonight.

BUDDY. Is she as pretty as the one that just left?

ALAN. Peggy? Prettier. With none of the disadvantages.

BUDDY. Boy, what a great place to live. And all for thirty bucks a month. (*Sits* R. C. *chair.*)

ALAN. (*Hangs up.*) Hey, that's right. I forgot we're sharing everything. How would you like to meet her? (*Crosses* R. *to him.*)

BUDDY. Who?

ALAN. Peggy. From upstairs.

BUDDY. (*Jumps up.*) Me? Are you kidding?

ALAN. Why? She's coming down anyway. No sense in sending her home empty-handed.

BUDDY. But she's expecting you.

ALAN. Turn the lights down low. She won't figure it out till she's going back up in the elevator.

BUDDY. You're crazy.

ALAN. No. That's how I met her. She rang the wrong bell one night. There's some poor guy in this building waiting for her since last July.

BUDDY. You're not serious, Alan. She probably baby-sits for boys like me.

ALAN. No. She's only twenty-two.

BUDDY. I'm talking about experience, not age. I didn't realize it until I got here tonight, but I've been living in a convent all my life.

ALAN. Buddy, trust me. She'll be crazy about you.

BUDDY. (*Crossing* L. *to coffee table,* R. *end.*) No, she won't. I don't want to meet her, Alan.

ALAN. (*Crossing* L. *to him.*) I don't get you. Where's your spirit of adventure? You sound like an old man.

BUDDY. An old man?

ALAN. Sure, look at the way you dress. Why does a young boy like you wear a black suit?

BUDDY. It's not black. It's charcoal gray.

ALAN. Whatever it is, you look like Herbert Hoover.

BUDDY. I'm sorry. I'll buy an all-white suit tomorrow.

ALAN. Buddy, I don't do this for everyone. Just brothers I love.

BUDDY. I'd like to, Alan, but gee, I had other plans. (*Breaks away* L. *of coffee table.*)

ALAN. What other plans?

BUDDY. (*Turns to him.*) They've got that emergency U.N. meeting on television tonight. I'd really like to see it.

ALAN. The U.N.? Buddy, if I offered this to the Security Council, the meeting would be off tonight.

BUDDY. Look, maybe you're not interested in what's going on in the world, but I am.

ALAN. I'm interested in what's going on with you. What is it? Are you afraid?

BUDDY. Yes—I mean, no.

ALAN. You mean, yes.

BUDDY. No, I don't.

34

ALAN. You know, something just occurred to me. Is it possible that—?

BUDDY. You're going to be late, Alan.

ALAN. I figured you were in the Army, overseas. Paris. I took it for granted—

BUDDY. (*Crosses up* L. *of sofa.*) I got around.

ALAN. Where? In a sightseeing bus?

BUDDY. What are you making such a fuss about? What's so damn important about it, anyway?

ALAN. (*Crosses* U. R. *of sofa.*) It's plenty important.

BUDDY. (*Evades him, crossing* D. R. *to* R. *counter.*) I'll get around to it soon enough.

ALAN. Buddy, baby, why didn't you tell me? (*Crosses* R. *to* BUDDY.) That's what big brothers are for. This is the answer to your problem.

BUDDY. (*Turns to him.*) I haven't got a problem.

ALAN. You haven't, huh?

BUDDY. Look, there's a big difference between the way you and I operate. If I get a handshake from a girl I figure I had a good night.

ALAN. With Peggy, all you have to do is say "Hello." From there on it's down hill.

BUDDY. It can't be that easy. I know. I've tried.

ALAN. Look kid, I wanted to get you a birthday present anyway. Now I found something you haven't got.

BUDDY. (*Turns front.*) I don't want it. I'm happy the way I am.

ALAN. Buddy, please. If not for your sake, then for mine.

BUDDY. (*Looks at him.*) For yours?

ALAN. Ever since I moved out, I felt I haven't really been looking after you—the way a big brother should. I want to make it up to you, kid.

BUDDY. I'm not complaining. You've been fine.

ALAN. It would really give me pleasure, Buddy, to do this for you. It's something a father could never do.

BUDDY. (*Front.*) I'll say.

ALAN. But brothers, well, it's different. Buddy—I feel that it's my duty and privilege to help you at this very important time of your life. What do you say, Buddy? Please!

35

BUDDY. (*To him.*) Well—if it'll make you happy, all right.

ALAN. Thanks, kid. (BUDDY *shrugs.* ALAN *crosses* L. *to phone, sits and dials;* BUDDY *crosses* R.) You'll see. This'll be set up so perfectly, you won't even have to say a word to her— (*Hums "In a Little Spanish Town." Into phone.*) Hello? Peggy?— Yeah— No, no, wait a minute— (*He rises.*) I have good and bad news— First the bad news. I've got to go out— No, most of the evening. Important business— You ready for the good news?— He's here— Manheim!

BUDDY. (*At counter* R.—*turns.*) Who?

ALAN. (*Into phone.*) Oscar Manheim, the producer from M.G.M.

BUDDY. (*Runs* L. *of* C.) *What?*

ALAN. Just as you left. He's staying in my apartment tonight— He wants to meet you.

BUDDY. I'm gonna get out of here. (*He points to door.*)

ALAN. (*Into phone.*) Yes, now— I told him all about you.

BUDDY. Please, Alan!

ALAN. (*Into phone.*) Ten minutes?— Fine— Oh, don't you dare thank me, honey. I'm really doing *him* the favor. (*He hangs up.*) The ball's over the fence, kid. All you've got to do now is run the bases.

BUDDY. Are you out of your mind? Me? A producer?

ALAN. You want to be a director? I'll call her back. (*Motions to phone.*)

BUDDY. But why did you tell her that?

ALAN. Just to make it easier for you.

BUDDY. Easier?

ALAN. (*Crosses to him.*) Now the pressure's off you. It's all on her.

BUDDY. What are you talking about?

ALAN. She's got a bug about getting into pictures. Now's her chance to prove how really talented she is.

BUDDY. How would I know?

ALAN. Because you're a big producer from MGM, Oscar Manheim.

BUDDY. Doesn't she know what he looks like?

ALAN. No. I made him up. Sounds real, huh?

BUDDY. Made it up? But she could call MGM and check.

ALAN. *She doesn't know how to dial.* Look. She's been auditioning for years without making a picture. She's got more money than MGM. She's having too much fun being discovered.

BUDDY. What am I supposed to do, make her a star?

ALAN. No. Just give her a small part in the picture.

BUDDY. *What picture??*

ALAN. "I Was a Teenage Producer." I don't know. Can't you make up a picture?

BUDDY. (*Breaking away* R., *sits* D. R. C. *chair.*) No. Right now I can't even think of my own name.

ALAN. (*Gets ready to leave, gets coat.*) You're my brother. When the chips are down, you'll come through.

BUDDY. A twenty-one-year-old movie producer. Holy cow! (*Crosses* L. *to sofa.*)

ALAN. (*Starts Upstage.*) Well, I'd better get going.

BUDDY. Wait a minute. When is she going to be here?

ALAN. Ten minutes. She just lives upstairs.

BUDDY. Ten minutes? I don't feel so good.

ALAN. (*Crosses* D. *to* R. *of sofa.*) Look, if you're really too scared I'll call her back and cancel it.

BUDDY. No. No, never mind.

ALAN. You won't admit it, but you're glad I called. Is there anything you need?

BUDDY. Yeah. A drink.

ALAN. Here you are. (*Hands drink to him from coffee table. Then picks up trench coat, starts Upstage.*)

BUDDY. Well, here's to Oscar Wilhelm.

ALAN. (*Turns back.*) *Manheim.*

BUDDY. Oh, jeez. (*He drinks it all quickly.*)

ALAN. Hey, take it easy with that stuff. (*Crossing up to foyer; puts on trench coat.*)

BUDDY. Can you imagine if I drop dead and she calls the police? They'll bury me in Hollywood.

ALAN. It's going to be the greatest night of your life. You'll thank me for it some day. (*He's at the door.*)

BUDDY. Alan!

ALAN. Yes?

BUDDY. Will you call before you come **home?**

ALAN. I'll call, I'll ring the doorbell and I'll cough loud as soon as I'm within two blocks of the house. (*He opens the door.*) So long, kid. And happy birthday! (*And he's gone, closing door.*)

BUDDY. (*He stares after him a minute.*) Happy birthday!— Why couldn't he get me a tie like everyone else?— How'd I get talked into this? (*He rubs his stomach as he apparently just got a twinge of nervousness. He picks up both glasses and puts them on bar. Starts R., above coffee table, gets a thought, looks at his own jacket. Runs up to hall closet, takes out jacket, looks at it, puts it back. Then he takes out a bright blue smoking jacket, runs down to sofa, throws hanger on sofa table and puts on smoking jacket. Picks up cigarette and starts to light it. As he does so DOORBELL rings. He stands paralyzed with fear. Screams.*) Oh!— Just a sec— (*He looks around in a panic. He starts Upstage, sees his jacket on sofa and throws it under back of sofa. Then he runs to the door and stops quickly to compose himself. He straightens himself up. Hell, he's going to go through with it. He opens the door. A small, rather harassed WOMAN in her late fifties stands there. He yells.*) Mom!

WOMAN. (*Crossing D. R., sits D. R. C. chair.*) Oh, darling, I'm so glad you're here.

BUDDY. (*Follows L. of her, in a state of shock.*) Mom!

CURTAIN FALLS

ACT TWO

TIME: *Immediately after.*

AT RISE: BUDDY *is frantically pacing back and forth.
BUDDY is about to have his first experience and here
sits his mother.* MRS. BAKER *is a woman who has
managed to find a little misery in the best of things.
Sorrow and trouble are the only things that can make
her happy. She was born in this country, dresses in
fine fashion and in general her speech and appearance
are definitely American. But she thinks old-world.
Superstitions, beliefs, customs still cling to her. Or
rather she clings to them. Because of this, we can't
take her hysterics too seriously. At rise* BUDDY
crosses R., *then* L., *then* R. *to her.*

BUDDY. (L. *of* MOTHER.) Mom, are you feeling all
right?

MOTHER. (*Seated* D. R. C. *chair.*) Darling, can I have a
cold glass of water? I almost fainted on the subway.

BUDDY. Mom, what are you doing here?

MOTHER. I got such a dizzy spell. I never thought I'd
get here.

BUDDY. Mom—what did you want?

MOTHER. A glass of water, sweetheart.

BUDDY. No, I meant— (*But maybe the water would be
quicker. He rushes* U. L. *to the bar and pours a glass of
water.*)

MOTHER. I've got no luck. I never had any and I never
will.

BUDDY. (*Rushes back* R. *with glass.*) Here, Mom.

MOTHER. (*Takes a sip.*) That just makes me nauseous.
(*He takes glass and puts it on fireplace bench* L.) Let me
catch my breath.

BUDDY. (*Crosses* D. *to* L. *of her.*) Maybe you need
some fresh air, Mom. Outside?

39

MOTHER. Just let me sit a few minutes— (*Rises.*) Where's Alan? (*Crosses* L. *of* C.)

BUDDY. (*Crosses* L., R. *of her.*) Out. On business. Do you feel any better?

MOTHER. (*Turns to him.*) When did I ever feel better?

BUDDY. Mom, I hope you understand, but I've got this appointment tonight.

MOTHER. Did you have dinner yet?

BUDDY. What? Dinner? Yes. Yes, I had a sandwich.

MOTHER. A sandwich? For supper? That's how you start the minute you're away?

BUDDY. I'm not hungry, Mom. You see, I've got this appointment—

MOTHER. What'd you have, one of those greasy hamburgers?

BUDDY. No. Roast beef. I had a big roast beef sandwich.

MOTHER. That's not enough for you. Let me make you some eggs. (*Starts* D. L.)

BUDDY. (*A step* L.) I don't want any eggs.

MOTHER. (*Fingers* D. L. *counter.*) Look at this place. Look at the dirt.

BUDDY. It's all right, Mom.

MOTHER. (*Turns to coffee table, looks down.*) Sure. Boys. I'll bet no one's been in here to clean in a year.

BUDDY. (*He might as well tell her.*) Mom, will you listen to me? I'm—I'm—I'm expecting a girl here in a few minutes.

MOTHER. (*Looking down at table.*) To clean?

BUDDY. (*Exasperated.*) No, not to clean— She's a friend of mine.

MOTHER. (*Looks at him.*) From our neighborhood?

BUDDY. (*Steps Downstage.*) No, you don't know her. She's—er—a girl I knew in school. We're writing a story together.

MOTHER. (*Starts* R.) Then let me make you some appetizers.

BUDDY. (*Stops her.*) We don't want any appetizers.

MOTHER. Buddy, I've got to talk to you about your father.

BUDDY. Can't we do it tomorrow? She's going to be here any second.

MOTHER. (*A whimper.*) What's the matter? She's more important than me?

BUDDY. (*Placating.*) Mom, no one's more important than you.

MOTHER. (*Cries.*) How can you say that when you worry me like this? I know you. You won't eat unless the food's in front of you.

BUDDY. (*Puzzled; breaks* R. *of* C.) *No one* eats unless the food's in front of them. Mom, I haven't got time— (*Turns to her.*)

MOTHER. (*Starts Upstage; hurt.*) You want me to go, I'll go.

BUDDY. Mom, please don't be hurt. I didn't want to have this meeting. It came up unexpectedly. But I have to go through with it.

MOTHER. Buddy, your father's going to be home in a few minutes. You should have heard him on the phone before about Alan. If the operator was listening, there'll be a man there in the morning to rip it off the wall!

BUDDY. I can't discuss this with you now.

MOTHER. No, but for girls you've got time. (*Crosses* D. R.; *sits* R. C. *chair; cries.*)

BUDDY. (*Crosses* D., R. *of* C.) It's not a girl. It's—a— meeting. (*Looks to door and back.*) About a story we're writing. It may go on till two o'clock in the morning.

MOTHER. Without appetizers?

BUDDY. *We don't need appetizers!*

MOTHER. (*Rises, crosses to him.*) Wait'll he reads that letter. Wait'll he finds out you're gone. Remember what he did when Alan left?

BUDDY. I know, Mom. He was very upset.

MOTHER. Upset? I'll never forget it. He came home from work at three o'clock, went into his room, put on his pajamas and got into bed to die. Four days he stayed in bed. He just laid there waiting to die.

BUDDY. But he didn't die, Mom. He put on weight.

MOTHER. Don't think he wasn't disappointed. He was plenty hurt by Alan leaving, believe me. He thought by now Alan would be married, have a grandchild. Who knows if he'll ever get married? And now you.

BUDDY. Mom, please—

MOTHER. I know what he's going to say tonight. He'll blame it all on me. He'll say I was too easy with the both of you. He'll say, "because of you my sister Gussie has two grandchildren and all I've got is a *bum*—and a *letter.*" I know him.

BUDDY. Look, Mom. How about if I come home to-morrow night for dinner? And I'll have a long talk with Dad about everything. Okay?

MOTHER. Tomorrow? By tomorrow he'll be in bed again writing out his will. He'll be on the phone saying good-bye to his family.

BUDDY. He won't, Mom. He just gets very dramatic sometimes.

MOTHER. (*Crosses* R., *sits* D. R. C. *chair.*) Maybe I am too easy-going. Maybe if I were like some mothers— (BUDDY *looks to door.*) who forbid their children to do everything, I'd be better off today.

BUDDY. No, Mom. You're the best mother I ever had— (*Crosses* R. *to her.*) Do you feel any better?

MOTHER. How do I know? I feel too sick to tell.

BUDDY. Really, a good night's sleep and you'll feel wonderful. Take something before you go to bed. Some warm milk.

MOTHER. (*Cries.*) Who buys milk now that you're not there?

BUDDY. (L. *of her.*) Then buy some.

MOTHER. Maybe I'll be better off if I take a hot bath.

BUDDY. That's the girl.

MOTHER. (*Front.*) I'll probably pass out right in the tub.

BUDDY. No, you won't. Why do you get so emotional all the time?

MOTHER. I don't look for it, believe me, darling. (*Pats his face.*)

BUDDY. Mom, everything's going to be all right? (*He half lifts her to her feet.* MOTHER *crosses* L. *in front of him to* C.) Sleep tight. (*He kisses her forehead.*)

42

MOTHER. I feel better knowing at least you'll be there tomorrow.

BUDDY. For dinner. I promise. (*He starts Upstage.*)

MOTHER. (*A turn up and back, she stops.*) What'll I make?

BUDDY. (*Coming down to her.*) What?

MOTHER. For dinner? What do you want to eat?

BUDDY. Anything. I don't care. Good night, Mom. (*Gestures to door.*)

MOTHER. I want to make something you like now that you're not home.

BUDDY. I like everything. Roast beef, okay?

MOTHER. All right, good. (*He starts Upstage. She starts, then stops.*) You had roast beef tonight.

BUDDY. (*He comes back; beside himself with anxiety.*) I can eat it again.

MOTHER. I could get a turkey. A big turkey.

BUDDY. Okay! Turkey! Wonderful!

MOTHER. It doesn't really pay for one night.

BUDDY. (*He can't take it any more. He practically screams, jumping up and down.*) Mom, for Pete's sakes, it doesn't matter.

MOTHER. (*Near tears.*) What are you yelling? I'm only trying to make you happy. Who do I cook for, myself? I haven't eaten anything besides coffee for ten years.

BUDDY. I'm sorry, Mom.

MOTHER. Oh— (*Crosses D. R. C., staggers, hand on heart. BUDDY helplessly holds out arms, swinging a step L. as she passes him.*) I've got that stick in the heart again. (*Sits R. C. chair. Pause.*)

BUDDY. You're just upset.

MOTHER. No. I ate lamb chops tonight. They never agree with me.

BUDDY. (*Exasperated; staggers L.*) Oh, boy.

MOTHER. Darling, do you have an alka-seltzer?

BUDDY. Alka-seltzer? I don't know— Wait a minute. I'll look in the kitchen. (*He rushes off madly to the kitchen R.*)

MOTHER. (*She rubs her stomach.*) She wished it on me. His sister Gussie wished it on me.

BUDDY. (*He comes running back out,* L. *of her.*) There isn't any here.

MOTHER. Sure. Boys. You wouldn't have water if you didn't have a faucet.

BUDDY. Mom, make anything you want. Turkey. Roast beef. I'll be home tomorrow night. Now, why don't you go home and relax? Take a cab.

MOTHER. It's starting to rain. Where am I going to get a cab?

BUDDY. I'll get you one, okay?

MOTHER. All right. Let me sit a few minutes.

BUDDY. A few minutes? (*He can't wait any longer.*) Mom, I'll get the doorman to get you a cab. (*Runs up to door.*) Do you want to wait in the lobby?

MOTHER. You don't have to run out.

BUDDY. I'll be right back. In two minutes. (*And he is gone in a flash; slams door.*)

MOTHER. Don't get overheated— Who am I talking to? (*She looks around the apartment and shakes her head disapprovingly. Puts bag on chair, unbuttons coat. She gets up, crosses to the coffee table, empties one ash tray into the other. Then starts to cross with the refuse into the kitchen* R. *when the PHONE rings. She turns and goes to the phone, above coffee table. Into phone.*) Hello? Who?— No, he isn't. To whom am I speaking to, please? Meltzer? Martin Meltzer— No, this is Alan's mother— What?—Why should I kid about a thing like that? No, I'm positive he's not here— A message?— Wait. I'll get a pencil. (*She looks for a pencil. There is none on the table, so she runs quickly to the* L. *cabinet, then Upstage cabinet, turns and gestures to phone as if saying, "I'm coming," then to sofa table and looks frantically for a pencil. There is none to be found. She runs back* R. *around sofa; quickly to the phone.*) Go on, I'll remember. Talk fast so I could write it down as soon as you're finished— "Extremely important. Your wife just came in unexpectedly from Atlantic City and is on her way to the Hotel Croyden so Alan should be sure *not* to come with those certain parties."— Yes, I have it— I do— I can't repeat it to you. I'm trying to remember it— Mr. Meltzer, Hotel Croyden— Yes. . . . Don't talk any more, I'm going to write it down quick. Good-bye. (*She hangs up.*) Some message. That's a book, not a message. (*She starts to look for a pencil again.*) Where's a pencil? (*She crosses* R. *toward counter.*) They don't have Alka-Seltzer, they're gonna have a pencil? (*The PHONE rings. She turns.*) Suddenly I'm an answering service. (*Crosses* L. *to phone, answers it.*) Hello?— No, he isn't— This is Alan's mother— Why should I kid about a thing like that?— To whom am I speaking to, please?— Who?— Chickie?— That's a name?— Chickie Parker— You forgot whose hotel?— Mr. Meltzer's? Where do I know that name from?— Oh, for God sakes, he just called. With a message to Alan. Something about Atlantic City. I think he said Alan shouldn't go there— I don't know what it means either. I'm not a secretary. I'm a mother—without a pencil— The hotel?— Yes, he did mention it— I think it was the Parker— Oh, that's *your* name— Wait. Oh, yes. The Croyden. . . . A message for Alan? (*Cries.*) I can only try, darling— "Chickie was detained but she's on her way to the Croyden now."— Yes. You're welcome. Good-bye. (*She hangs up.*) There must be some carrying on here. (*Crosses Upstage to desk.*) Their father should only know— A businessman and a college boy and they don't have a pencil. (*She starts* R. *and the PHONE rings again.*) Oh, for God's sake. (*The PHONE rings again.*) All right, all right, what do you want from me? (*She rushes quickly to the phone and picks it up.*) Yes?— Who?— Who did you want, please?—No, he's out. This is Alan's mother— Listen, don't start that with me— Who is this?— Connie what?— Again with a message— Miss, can't you write it down? I don't have a pencil— You what?— Yes— Yes— Yes— You're welcome— Good-bye. (*She hangs up.*) Good-bye, go home, good luck, who knows what she said? (*Sits sofa and cries.*) Who tells him to have so many phone calls?— It's disgusting. (*The PHONE rings. She screams.*) What do you want from my life? (*She just stares at the phone. It continues to ring.*) Oh, I'm so nauseous. (*She can't stand it any longer. She rises, picks it up, but she yells at it angrily.*) Hello?— What do you want?— Who is this?—Alan who?— Oh, Alan. . . .

(*She starts to cry.*) It's Mother. (*She sits.*) What am I doing here? I'm answering your phone calls— He's outside getting me a subway— I mean a taxi— No, there's no one else here— Who called?—The whole world called— First a man called— Meltzer?— No, it didn't sound like that—

BUDDY. (*The door opens and he rushes in; closes door. Crosses* D. C., R. *of her.*) Okay, Mom.

MOTHER. (*Into phone.*) Oh, I've got to go now. Buddy is here with the cab. Talk to Buddy.

BUDDY. I've got the cab. It's waiting outside.

MOTHER. Here. (*Hands him phone.*)

BUDDY. Who is that?

MOTHER. Alan. (*She gets up and hands phone to* BUDDY *and crosses* R. *to get bag.*)

BUDDY. (*Taking phone; steps* L. *above table.*) Hello, Alan?— What's wrong? I don't know who called, I was outside. (*To* MOTHER.) Mom, did someone call?

MOTHER. (*Crosses to* C.) I gave all the messages to Alan. I don't want to keep the taxi waiting. Good-bye, sweetheart. (*She starts to door.*)

BUDDY. Mom, who called? A girl?

MOTHER. (*Turns on top step.*) Yes, darling. Good-bye. (*Turns Upstage.*)

BUDDY. What did she say?

MOTHER. (*Turns.*) I don't remember. (*Turns, opens door.*)

BUDDY. Why didn't you write it down?

MOTHER. (*Crosses* D. *to edge of foyer.*) Don't *you* start with me— This must be costing a fortune. I only hope I don't pass out in the taxi! (*She goes, slamming the door.*)

BUDDY. Mom, wait— (*Into phone.*) Hello, Allen— I don't know. I can't make head or tail out of her— Where are you?— No, she didn't get here yet— Lousy, that's how I feel— I already had a drink. It doesn't help— Hey, wait a minute. Who am I again?— Oscar *Wol*heim?— *Manheim!* Oscar Manheim— Oh, boy! Look, Alan. I changed my mind. I can't go through with it. I'm going out. Yes, now. Well— I'll leave her a note from you— I'm sorry. Good-bye. (*He hangs up.*) That's it. I'll leave her a note. That's all. (*He quickly starts to search for a pencil and paper. He crosses* U. R. *of sofa, looks sofa table, crosses* L. *to bar counter, then looks in the shelves under* D. L. *cabinet and takes out container with two dozen pencils. He crosses to table behind sofa and finds piece of paper. He sits sofa and starts to write and repeats aloud.*) "Dear Peggy— More bad news— Oscar— (*Momentarily forgets name.*) —Manheim—is— dead!— Love— Alan." (*He puts down pencil, then crosses to door. Reads letter again. As he bends down to leave it under door, the DOORBELL rings. He gasps. The BELL rings again. He throws up his hands in despair and then opens door.* PEGGY *stands there, ravishingly dressed. She looks utterly fantastic.*)

PEGGY. Hi. I'm Peggy Evans. (*She walks in, crosses* D. L. *He closes door.*) I'm not disturbing you or anything, am I?

BUDDY. (*He looks at her, overwhelmed by her pulchritude, follows her* D. R., L. *of* D. R. C. *chair.*) No—not at all. (*He is in a state of semi-shock.*)

PEGGY. (*Sitting on sofa,* R. *end.*) Alan said you wanted to meet me. I hope you forgive the way I look. I've been in a car all day—I must be a mess.

BUDDY. No— You look—very neat. (*He tears up the note and puts the pieces in his pocket.*)

PEGGY. Thanks. Coming from you, that's something. (*She crosses to him.*) It's a shame you couldn't get up to the ski lodge.

BUDDY. (*Backs away a step; frightened.*) What ski lodge?

PEGGY. In New Hampshire. Or Vermont. I'm not very good at names. In fact, I'm afraid I've forgotten yours.

BUDDY. Oh— It's—*Man*heim.

PEGGY. That's right. Mr. Manheim.

BUDDY. *Jack* Man—Heim.

PEGGY. Yes, I remember the "Jack."

BUDDY. (*A take.*) Oh? Won't you sit down? (*Indicating* R. C. *chair.*)

PEGGY. Thank you. (*Crosses* L. *and sits on sofa; he looks frightened.*) I understand you had some problem at the studio.

47

BUDDY. Oh, yes—we did.

PEGGY. What was it? (*She takes a cigarette and lights it.*)

BUDDY. It was—er— (*Stymied, then he sees flame.*) Er—we had a—fire. (*Crosses L. to C.*)

PEGGY. Who?

BUDDY. I beg your pardon?

PEGGY. Who did you have to fire?

BUDDY. No, no. *A* fire. Part of the studio burned down.

PEGGY. Oh? Was anyone hurt?

BUDDY. No—just a few extras— Say, would you like a drink?

PEGGY. Ooooh, like a transfusion. I don't mind admitting it, but I'm nervous.

BUDDY. *You're* nervous? What would you like?

PEGGY. What are you having?

BUDDY. (*This one is easy. He tosses it off grandly.*) Oh— Scotch and ginger ale.

PEGGY. Oh, that's cute. I mean what are you *really* having?

BUDDY. (*Embarrassed.*) I don't know. What are you having?

PEGGY. Grand Marnier.

BUDDY. Grandma who?

PEGGY. Grand Marnier. It's French. You know, a liquoor.

BUDDY. Oh— (*He crosses U. L. to bar and looks for it. He picks up a Scotch bottle.*) No, I don't see any.

PEGGY. Oh, Scotch'll be fine. (BUDDY *pours drinks.*) I suppose you've heard it before, but you look awfully young for a producer.

BUDDY. (*Crossing L. of her.*) Oh, do I?

PEGGY. To look at you I'd say you were only about 26, but I bet I'm way off.

BUDDY. Oh, way off. (*Hands her drink and sits L. of her.*) Well, here we are.

PERRY. What should we drink to?

BUDDY. Anything you like.

PEGGY. Let's make a silent toast.

BUDDY. Okay.

(They both close their eyes, take a beat. She opens hers, nudges him, he opens his eyes, clink glasses and drink. He makes a face at the straight whiskey.)

PEGGY. *(Makes herself comfortable, puts down glass and snuffs out cigarette.)* Well, now—down to business.

BUDDY. *(A take.)* Huh?

PEGGY. I suppose you want to know what I've done.

BUDDY. *(Stalling.)* Not necessarily.

PEGGY. I'll be perfectly frank with you. I've never been in a picture before.

BUDDY. Is that so?

PEGGY. But I'm not totally inexperienced.

BUDDY. *(Straight.)* So Alan told me.

PEGGY. Last summer when I was on the coast I did an "Untouchables."

BUDDY. No kidding?

PEGGY. I was a dead body. They fished me out of the river.

BUDDY. I think I saw that.

PEGGY. Lots of people did. I got loads of work from it. But it's not what I really want to do. That's why I'm taking acting class. With Felix Ungar. He lives in this building. Right under this apartment. In fact *that's* how I met Alan. *(She puts her hand on his knee.)* I rang the wrong bell one night.

BUDDY. *(He looks down at his knee and laughs almost hysterically.)* How about that?

PEGGY. And look how it turned out. Through a silly mistake, I'm being auditioned by one of the biggest producers— *(Taking hand off knee.)* in the business. Life is funny, isn't it?

BUDDY. *(Puts drink down and rises, crossing* R.*)* Hysterical. *(Crosses* R. *of* C.*)*

PEGGY. *(Rises, crosses below coffee table.)* Well, is there anything you'd like me to do?

BUDDY. *(Turns quickly.)* What?

PEGGY. Do. Read a scene? Or kind of take on a character like in class. Or is just talking like this enough?

BUDDY. Oh, it's plenty. To tell the truth, I'm a little tired. *(Sits* R. C. *chair.)*

PEGGY. (*Crosses* R. *to* C.) Oh, from the trip. Would you like me to massage your think muscle?

BUDDY. Huh?

PEGGY. Here! (*She indicates her temple. She goes to where he's sitting, and stands over him.*) Just close your eyes and put your head back.

BUDDY. I don't think—

PEGGY. I'm very good at this. Now just relax— (*He does.*) and try and forget about the picture business. (*She massages.*) No, I can feel it. You're still thinking about the studio.

BUDDY. (*As a silly grin slowly breaks on his face.*) No, I'm not. I swear I'm not.

(*The BUZZER rings.* BUDDY *jumps up.*)

PEGGY. Are you expecting anyone?

BUDDY. Me? No! No! (*It rings again, angrily.*) No, I'll get it. I'll get it. (*He crosses to house phone quickly and picks it up. Into phone.*) Hello?— *Dad!*— I'm sorry. I didn't mean to yell— What?— Now?— Look, Dad, I'll come downstairs, okay?— Dad?— Dad?— Oh, boy! (*He hangs up, crosses* D. *to* L. *of* C.)

PEGGY. (*Steps* L. *to* C.) Is anything wrong?

BUDDY. (*Turns to her.*) What? Oh, yeah— It's—it's someone I don't want to see— A writer—

PEGGY. Dad? It sounded like it was your father.

BUDDY. Oh! Oh, no. That's just a nickname. Dad. You know, like Ernest Hemingway is Poppa.

PEGGY. Oh! Is Dad coming up?

BUDDY. Yeah, Dad's coming up— Look, would you do me a big favor? I've got to be alone with him for a few minutes— To talk about script changes.

PEGGY. I understand. I could go up and get that bottle of Grand Marnier.

BUDDY. (*That's inspirational.*) That's it. Would you do that?

PEGGY. Of course. (*She starts for the door.*)

BUDDY. (*He stops her.*) Not that way!

PEGGY. What?

BUDDY. I don't want him to know I'm auditioning someone else. He's already got someone in mind.

PEGGY. Oh, I appreciate that. Thanks an awful lot, Mr. Manheim.

(*She kisses him and exits through the kitchen door. He starts R. to make sure she has gone. He looks at his jacket, unbuttons it, takes it off, throws it into bedroom and closes door. He runs Downstage, grabs the two glasses from coffee table and crosses L. and puts them on bar. He starts R., stops, looks at glasses. Picks one up and examines it for lipstick, takes out his handkerchief, wipes lipstick off, puts glass on bar. As he wipes his own mouth with handkerchief, DOORBELL rings. He frantically tries to jam handkerchief into pocket and can't. DOORBELL rings again. Panicky, he throws handkerchief out window L. He grabs a large book from Upstage bookshelf, opens it, goes to door, book in hand, composes himself as if he had been reading all evening and opens door. There stands his FATHER, with the letter in his hand.*)

BUDDY. Hello, Dad. (*The FATHER walks in, holds up the letter to BUDDY's face, to indicate he got it, then he walks into the apartment. BUDDY follows D. R. C., L. of him.*) Are you all right, Dad? Is anything wrong? (*The FATHER stares ahead speechless. He has taken letter out of envelope and now holds it in front of BUDDY's face.*) I—I didn't think you'd be coming down tonight. I was going to have a long talk with you in the morning—at the plant—and then I told mother I'd be home for dinner tomorrow—so you and I could sit down and talk some more—and I could explain how I— Dad, you're angry, aren't you. . . .

FATHER. Me? Angry. Why should I be angry?

BUDDY. About the letter.

FATHER. (*Looks at him.*) What letter?

BUDDY. This letter. The letter I wrote you.

FATHER. No, no. You didn't write this letter. Someone

51

I don't know wrote this letter. Not you. You, I know. This person I never met.

BUDDY. Dad, don't you think it would be better if we waited until tomorrow, when we're both—calmer? I meant to have a long talk with you about this.

FATHER. Talk? What's there to talk about? (*He still holds up letter.*) It's signed, sealed and delivered. The Declaration of Independence. What's there to talk about?

BUDDY. Dad, I think you're too upset now to discuss this logically.

FATHER. Oh, I expected it. (*Puts letter in envelope; crosses* R. *below* D. R. C. *chair.*) You hang around your brother long enough, it was bound to happen. So what's the windup. My sister Gussie has two grandchildren and I have a bum and a letter.

BUDDY. (*Crosses* R. *to him.*) Dad, this didn't suddenly happen. I tried to explain how I felt the other night. But you wouldn't listen.

FATHER. I wouldn't listen! (*He starts to sit and jumps up.*) Don't try and tell me I wouldn't listen. That's all I did was listen. (*Crosses* L. *of* BUDDY *to sofa.*)

BUDDY. (*Turns.*) But every time I would start to say something, you would walk out of the room.

FATHER. (*Crossing to* L. *of* C.) If you showed me a little respect, then maybe I would listen.

BUDDY. Dad, you're not making any sense.

FATHER. (*Turns to him.*) *I'm* not making sense? Very nice. Very nice talk to a father.

BUDDY. What do you want me to say?

FATHER. (*Crosses* R. *to him.*) I want to hear from your own lips—nicely—why such a young boy can't live at home with his parents.

BUDDY. Young boy?

FATHER. (*Holding up a warning finger.*) *Nicely!*

BUDDY. Dad, I'm twenty-one.

FATHER. (*Non-committal; turns front.*) You're twenty-one.

BUDDY. You say it as if you don't believe me. I was twenty-one yesterday, wasn't I?

FATHER. (*Shrugs.*) Whatever you say.

BUDDY. What do you mean whatever I say?

FATHER. (*Finger up again.*) Nicely!

BUDDY. All right. *I say* I was twenty-one. That's old enough to make your own decisions in life. When *you* were twenty-one, you were already married, weren't you?

FATHER. You were there?

BUDDY. No, I wasn't there. You told me yourself.

FATHER. Those days were altogether different. (*Crosses away L. of sofa.*) I was working when I was eleven years old. (*Turns to him.*) *I* didn't go to camp.

BUDDY. *What's camp got to do with all this?*

FATHER. (*Threatening.*) I'll walk right out of here!

BUDDY. All right, Dad. I don't mean to be disrespectful, but your answers never match my questions.

FATHER. (*Crossing above and R. of sofa and of BUDDY.*) Oh, that too? I don't talk fancy enough for you like your brother and his show business friends.

BUDDY. (*Turns R.*) That's what I mean. Who said anything about show business?

FATHER. (R. *of* C.) Well, that's where he is all day, isn't he? Backstage at some burlesque house.

BUDDY. They haven't had burlesque in New York in twenty years.

FATHER. He hasn't put in a day's work in twenty years. (*Crosses D. R. of C.*) And now I suppose I can expect that of you.

BUDDY. No, Dad. I'll work there as long as you want me to—no matter how I feel about it.

FATHER. (*Turns, a step L.*) What do you mean, no matter how you feel?

BUDDY. Well, Dad, I never had a chance to try anything else. I had two years of college, then the Army and then right into the business. Maybe it's not the right field for me.

FATHER. Not the right field? (*Turns, looks at D. R. C. chair, then at BUDDY, and then crosses R. to chair. He addresses an imaginary listener in R. C. chair.*) I give the boy the biggest artificial fruit manufacturing house in the east, he tells me *not the right field*. Ha! That's a hot one. (*He sits R. C. chair.*)

BUDDY. I don't know if I've got any talent—but—I've always toyed with the idea of becoming a writer.

FATHER. A writer? What kind of writer? Letters? (*He holds up letter.*) Letters you write beautiful. I don't know who's going to buy them but they're terrific.

BUDDY. But supposing I'm good? I'm not even getting a chance to find out. Supposing I could write plays—for television or the theater?

FATHER. Plays can close. (*Crossing to him.*) Television you turn off. Wax fruit lays in the bowl till you're a hundred.

BUDDY. But business doesn't stimulate me, Dad. I don't have fun.

FATHER. You don't have fun? I'll put in music, you can dance while you work. (*Turns away R., shrugging.*)

BUDDY. Dad, forget about the business for now. I'll stay. All I want now is your permission for me to live here on my own. (*Crosses away L. a step.*)

FATHER. (*Puts letter in coat pocket. Crosses L. to him.*) All right, let me ask you a question. If you were in my place, if you were my father, with conditions in the world as they are today, with juvenile delinquency, with the stories you read in the papers about the crazy parties that go on, the drinking and what not—(*Loud.*) would you let *your* son leave home?

BUDDY. Yes!

FATHER. (*Quietly.*) That's no answer!

BUDDY. Dad, it just doesn't seem as if we're ever going to understand each other.

FATHER. (*Breaks R.*) How can we? You listen to your brother more than you listen to me.

BUDDY. That's not true.

FATHER. (*Turns, crosses to him.*) Do you deny that he's the one who put this bug in your mouth about leaving home?

BUDDY. In your ear, Dad.

FATHER. What?

BUDDY. Bug in your ear.

FATHER. (*Doffs his hat.*) Excuse my ignorance, Mr. Writer.

BUDDY. I wasn't making fun of you.

FATHER. (*Crosses away R.*) Why not? Your brother does.

BUDDY. No, he doesn't.

FATHER. He doesn't, heh? I can imagine the things he must tell you. (*Crosses* L. *to him.*) You'll learn plenty from him, believe me, plenty. At least you I had hopes for. Alan I could never talk to. But you, you were always good. I could take you anywhere. I could take you visiting, you would sit on a chair for three hours, (*Front.*) you wouldn't hear a peep out of you. I remember I used to say, give Aunt Gussie a kiss. You'd go right over and give Aunt Gussie a kiss. But the older one. I chased him all over Brooklyn one day because he wouldn't give Aunt Gussie a kiss— (*Turns to* BUDDY.) What was so terrible to give Aunt Gussie a kiss?

BUDDY. I guess it was that hat she wore. You always had to kiss her through a veil.

FATHER. (*Crosses away* R.) You see how you take his side?

BUDDY. I wasn't taking his side.

FATHER. (*Turns, looks at him.*) No, heh? What's the use talking to you? You'll do what he says in the end anyway. If you want to become a bum like him, that's your affair.

BUDDY. Why is Alan a bum?

FATHER. Is he married?

BUDDY. No.

FATHER. Then he's a bum! (*Sits* R. C. *chair.*)

BUDDY. Dad, you really never had any problems with me before, have you? Won't you trust me now? (*Crosses* R. *to him.*)

FATHER. (*Sighs.*) All right, you want trust. I'll give you trust.

BUDDY. What do you mean?

FATHER. There's a disagreement here. A dispute. We'll arbitrate.

BUDDY. That's all I've been asking of you.

FATHER. I've heard your side. You've heard my side. If you want, we'll give it a six month trial period. Fairer than that, I can't be.

BUDDY. I think that's very fair, Dad. **Six months is fine.** (*Crossing* L. *to sofa.*)

55

FATHER. Then it's settled. You'll come home and live for six months—

BUDDY. (*Yells, turns* C.) Come home? (*Shouts, crossing to him.*) You don't want to give me a trial. You don't want to be fair— You just—just—

FATHER. (*Rises and shakes hand.*) Don't you raise your voice. You're not too big to get a good slap across the face.

BUDDY. I'm sorry, Dad.

FATHER. I never thought I'd live to see this day. That a son would talk to his father like this. I've been some terrible father to you, haven't I?

BUDDY. No, Dad. You've been a wonderful father. Just meet me half way. Please—what do you say?

FATHER. (*Crosses* L. *of him.*) I'll—I'll let you know.

BUDDY. What do you mean, you'll let me know?

FATHER. (*Turns.*) I'm not rushing into any decisions hell mell— I'll go home and think about it. If you want, you can stay here tonight, I won't argue. But tomorrow, you'll come home for dinner and we'll see what we'll see.

BUDDY. All right, that'll be fine. Good night, Dad. (*He starts Upstage.*)

FATHER. You need any money?

BUDDY. No, I've got plenty. (*Comes back.*)

FATHER. Where are you going to sleep?

BUDDY. On the sofa.

FATHER. (*Looks.*) That's some place to sleep.

BUDDY. Dad, I'll be all right. I'll see you tomorrow. I promise.

FATHER. You don't have to promise. You say you'll be there, I trust you.

BUDDY. Thanks, Dad. Good night. (*Starts up again.*)

FATHER. (*Just about to leave, when he stops and turns.*) Oh, wait a minute.

BUDDY. (*Panicky.*) What's the matter?

FATHER. I want to call your mother. Tell her everything's all right. I know she's worried. (*He crosses to phone.*)

BUDDY. (*Crosses and sits* D. C. *chair.*) Oh, boy!

FATHER. (*He dials, sighing. Into phone.*) Hello?— Jezebel?— Is Mrs. Baker home?— Oh! I wonder where she is?— Listen, Jezebel, before you go home I want you to write down a message for her— All right, *get* a pencil—

(*Suddenly* PEGGY *comes out from the kitchen* R. *She wears a topcoat.* BUDDY *rises as she enters.*)

PEGGY. (D. R.) Excuse me, but I'm all out of Grand Marnier too, I'll run down to the liquor store and get some. (*To* FATHER.) Hello, Dad! (*She goes back out kitchen door. The* FATHER *stares after her dumbfounded.* BUDDY *is in a state of shock. The* FATHER *turns slowly back to the phone.*)

FATHER. Hello, Jezebel?— Tell Mrs. Baker I'm with the bum!— The twenty-one year old bum! (*He slams the phone down, crosses* R. *to* C., *turns and points an accusing finger at* BUDDY.) Bum!

BUDDY. (R. *of* C.) Dad—

FATHER. Bum!

BUDDY. Let me explain—

FATHER. Bum!

BUDDY. Please—

FATHER. Twenty-one years old! You're a bigger bum than your brother is right now and you've still got twelve years to go!

BUDDY. Dad, please.

(*The front door suddenly opens.* ALAN *walks in and sees the* FATHER.)

ALAN. Dad!!

FATHER. Ah, the other bum. Come on in. We're having a party. (BUDDY *sits* D. R. C. *chair.*)

ALAN. (*Crosses* D. R. *of* FATHER.) What are you doing here?

FATHER. I was invited to dinner. That's some cook you have in there.

ALAN. (*To* BUDDY.) Where?

BUDDY. (*Defeated.*) In the kitchen.

ALAN. What? (*To* BUDDY.) Well, didn't you explain? That she was waiting for me?

FATHER. I don't need you to make up stories. (*Crosses*

to BUDDY, R. *of* ALAN.) I've got Tennessee Williams for that. (*Doffs hat.*)

(*The PHONE rings.* FATHER *starts out.*)

ALAN. Dad, wait. I want to talk to you. (*He crosses* L. *quickly to the phone.*)

FATHER. I've heard enough. (*He starts to go, Upstage.*)

ALAN. (*Into phone.*) Hello?— Oh, Mr. Meltzer.

FATHER. (*Stops, on foyer.*) Meltzer? What does he want?

ALAN. (*Into phone.*) Now, please. Calm down. I tried to explain. There was a mixup somewhere.

FATHER. What's wrong?

ALAN. Nothing, Dad. Nothing. (*Into phone.*) What?— Well, how should I know your wife was coming in?— I didn't get any message from my mother.

FATHER. (*Crosses* D. *to him,* R. *of him.*) What are you talking about?

ALAN. (*Into phone.*) If I can just talk to your wife— Mr. Meltzer, there's no need for a lawsuit.

FATHER. Lawsuit? What lawsuit?

ALAN. Dad, wait a minute— (*Into phone.*) Mr. Meltzer—

FATHER. Give me that phone. (*Grabs phone and brightly says.*) Hello? Meltzer? This is Mr. Baker, senior. What's the trouble?

ALAN. He's hysterical, Dad. Don't listen to him.

FATHER. Your wife and *who* rang the doorbell together? What French girl?— But who arranged such a thing?— I see— (*Turns to* ALAN.) I see— Good-bye. (*He hands phone to* ALAN, *who hangs up. He starts for the door.* ALAN *follows* L. *of him, off steps.*)

ALAN. Dad, if you'd just listen for five minutes— Dad! Please say something!

(*The* FATHER *crosses past them in silence. He turns on raised foyer and speaks calmly.* BUDDY R. *of foyer off steps.*)

FATHER. May you and your brother live and be well.

58

God bless you, all the luck in the world, you should know nothing but happiness. If I ever speak to either one of you again, my tongue should fall out! (*He opens the door and goes, slamming door.*)

(*The* Two Brothers *stand there looking at each other helplessly.*)

Buddy. (*Crosses* R. *to fireplace.*) I knew it. I knew this would happen.

Alan. (*Concerned.*) Do you think he means it? (*Takes off coat and puts it on* L. *hand-rail.*)

Buddy. Means it? In ten minutes he'll be home, giving the rest of my clothes to the janitor.

Alan. (*Crosses* D. R. *of sofa.*) I never saw him this mad. Not since the day he chased me all over Brooklyn when I wouldn't give Aunt Gussie a kiss. (*Sits* R. *arm.*)

Buddy. Oh, he's mad all right. And he means it. (*Crosses* L. *to him.*) We're fired.

Alan. (*Musing.*) But how can he get along without us?

Buddy. And he was almost out the door. And then that fruit cake walks in and says "Hello, Dad." His moustache almost fell off.

Alan. I'm sorry, kid. I didn't mean to get you involved.

Buddy. It's not your fault.

Alan. I thought I was doing you a favor. Well, it's over with anyway.

Buddy. What's over? She's coming back with a French bottle to do silly little things.

Alan. She is?

Buddy. (*Crosses* L. *to him.*) She gets me all crazy. Suppose I do something nutty, like signing her to a five-year contract? (*DOORBELL rings.*) I can't face her again, Alan. Please.

Alan. All right, never mind. I'll take over. Go on out to a movie.

Buddy. (*Grabs his coat from under sofa, crosses to above* R. C. *chair.*) That's a great idea. Maybe one of my pictures is playing around.

(*DOORBELL rings again.* BUDDY *exits through kitchen* R. ALAN *opens door;* CONNIE *stands there with valise.*)

ALAN. Connie! (*Closes door. She puts down case and gives* ALAN *a long kiss interrupting his "Wha—," then when she releases him.*)

CONNIE. Me no Connie. Me Jane. You Tarzan. Jane come to swing with Tarzan in tree.

ALAN. What's in that suitcase?

CONNIE. The rest of my merchandise. (*She takes off her coat. Puts it on* R. *hand-rail with purse.*)

ALAN. Are you drunk?

CONNIE. On one martini?

ALAN. (*Crossing away* R. *above* R. C. *chair.*) You get loaded just ordering one.

CONNIE. Now, then, the bedroom. It's in that direction, isn't it? (*She picks up suitcase and starts for bedroom.*)

ALAN. You stay out of there. What's come over you?

CONNIE. Nothing, darling. I gave you a choice and you made it.

ALAN. What?

CONNIE. Wonderful service, isn't it? You don't even have to pick it up. We deliver.

ALAN. You're not drunk. You're crazy.

CONNIE. (*Puts down suitcase and crosses* R., *stalking him as he backs away* R.) Just think of it, darling! We're going to live together, love together. Fun, fun, fun. Sin, sin, sin.

ALAN. (*At* R. *counter.*) Connie, you're scaring the hell out of me.

CONNIE. (L. *of him.*) You don't even have to say you love me. And when you get bored, just kick me out and give me a letter of recommendation.

ALAN. Will you cut it out? It's not funny any more. (*Breaks away* L.)

CONNIE. I don't understand, Alan. Isn't this what you want? Isn't this what you asked for?

ALAN. No.

CONNIE. No.

ALAN. (L. *of* C.) That's right, no. I said I could see

nothing wrong for two young people who were very fond of each other to have a healthy, normal relationship. But I see no reason to turn this affair into a—foreign art movie.

CONNIE. Good heavens, sir. I must be in the wrong apartment.

ALAN. Look, I told you before. I'm not denying anything. Six nights a week I'm Leonard Lover. But with you—well, you're different.

CONNIE. (*A step* L. *to* R. C. *chair.*) Careful, Alan. You're on the brink of committing yourself.

ALAN. Who's keeping it a secret? I love you.

CONNIE. You weren't very sure.

ALAN. I am now. If I can turn down an offer like this with a girl like you, I must be in love.

CONNIE. Well, then—where does that leave us?

ALAN. (*Turns front.*) I don't know.

CONNIE. (*Sits* R. *arm of* R. C. *chair.*) You don't know?

ALAN. (*Crossing to her.*) Look, honey, you've got to give me a chance to think. A lot of things have happened tonight. I just lost my job.

CONNIE. I thought you worked for your father.

ALAN. We must be in a hell of a recession. He just let two sons go— Oh, Connie, don't you see—

CONNIE. No, I don't see. You love me but you won't marry me, and you love me too much to live with me.

ALAN. (*Crosses around chair to* R. *of it.*) I know. I can't figure it out either.

CONNIE. (*Angry.*) I see. Well, I'm sorry, Alan, but I can't spend the rest of my life waiting in the hallway. (*She gets up and crosses to* C.)

ALAN. Wait a minute.

CONNIE. (*Turns* C.) For what? I either come in or go out. You want me or you don't. Yes or no.

ALAN. Why can't things be like they were before?

CONNIE. It's too late. We've raised the stakes.

ALAN. Who made you the dealer all of a sudden?

CONNIE. If the game is too big, Alan, get out.

ALAN. I see. A brilliant maneuver, General. You've got me cornered. Very well, I surrender.

CONNIE. I don't take prisoners. (*She goes to foyer, gets purse.*)

ALAN. (*Crosses to R. end steps; angry.*) I mean it. If that's what you want, I'll marry you.

CONNIE. (*Grabs coat. Puts over L. arm.*) If that's the way you'll marry me, I don't want it.

ALAN. (*Crossing to her.*) Connie, wait. Where are you going?

CONNIE. (*Putting on coat.*) Right now I want to be about a thirty-five *dollar* taxi ride away from you.

ALAN. (*Sincerely. Crossing to her.*) Connie, wait—I don't want you to leave.

CONNIE. (*She's made up her mind.*) I'm sorry.

ALAN. You mean I won't see you again?

CONNIE. I don't know. Maybe if you get lonely enough. (*The PHONE rings.*) You probably won't have much chance tonight. Start in the morning. (*PHONE rings again.* CONNIE *picks up suitcase.*)

ALAN. Connie, wait.

CONNIE. Answer your phone, Alan. It's the second platoon. (*PHONE rings again.*)

ALAN. (*Crosses* D. L. C.; *picks up phone.*) Hello— Oh, Mom. (*To* CONNIE.) Connie, it's my mother.

CONNIE. Your mother? Oh, come on, Alan. (*She opens door.*)

ALAN. Why should I kid about a thing like that?

CONNIE. Good-bye. (*And she's gone, closing the door behind her.*)

ALAN. Connie— Connie, wait. (*Back into phone. He sits.*) Hello, Mom?— What's wrong? Did Dad get home yet?— Aunt Gussie's?— Well, don't worry about it. He'll probably just sleep there tonight. He'll be home tomorrow when he calms down— Mom, please don't cry. . . . All right, look, I'll come up and sleep there tonight— Yes, in my old room— I don't feel like being alone either— What?— No, not yet— Mom, please, I'm very upset— I've got a lot on my mind— I can't decide that now— Mom, I don't care—lamb chops, turkey, chicken salad, anything—

CURTAIN

ACT THREE

Time: *Three weeks later.*

At Rise: Buddy *has Alan's sports jacket in his arms, one sleeve draped over his shoulder. The jacket is putting in extra duty as Buddy's dancing partner. This is a different Buddy than the one we've seen before. In a few weeks he seems to have blossomed. He now has the assurance and self-confidence that come with independence. He has a bounce and vitality we haven't seen before. Clothing is strewn around apartment. Buddy dances and chants his own rhythm.*

Buddy. (d. r., *dancing.*) One, two, cha-cha-cha— Very good, cha-cha-cha— And turn, cha-cha-cha. (*The TELEPHONE rings on "turn."*) Answer phone, cha-cha-cha— Very good, cha-cha-cha— (*He places coat on sofa saying "Excuse me, my dear." He picks up phone.*) Hello?— Snow? (*He sits sofa.*) Don't you know you could get arrested for having such a sexy voice?— No— I'm still trying to get tickets for the Ionesco play that's opening tonight— They're supposed to call me. Then I thought we might go up to the Palladium—for a little cha-cha-cha. Oh, say, could you pick me up here? It would be easier— Wonderful— 42 East 63rd Street. About seven? —Make it five to. I'm only human— Good-bye. (*He hangs up, slaps his hands, and gives a little giggle of joy. Then he resumes; dances l.*) Do it right, cha-cha-cha— Tonight's the night, cha-cha-cha . . . (*The PHONE rings. He picks it up. Sits on Upstage end of coffee table.*) Hello? (*At this moment, the door opens and Alan enters. Or better, he drags in. This is not the Alan of two weeks ago. He looks bedraggled. He seems to have lost a great deal of cockiness, his self-assurance. He hangs trench coat in closet and crosses d. r. to counter, picks up Fig Newton box, finds it empty, puts it down.*) Yes, it is— Yes?— Oh, wonderful— That's two tickets for tonight— Yes, I'll

63

pick them up at the box office— In Alan Baker's name— Thank you very much. Good-bye. (*He hangs up; sees* ALAN.) Oh, hi, Aly. I didn't hear you come in. (*Crosses to* C.) Gee, what a break. Your broker just got me two tickets for the Ionesco play tonight. I used your name. Is it all right?

ALAN. (*Staring ahead.*) Why not? I'm not using it any more. (*Sits* R. *bar stool.*)

BUDDY. (*He picks up his dancing partner, and resumes* C.) And again, cha-cha-cha— To the right, cha-cha-cha— (*He keeps on dancing.*) Where were you today?

ALAN. (*Staring ahead.*) At the Polo Grounds waiting for the Giants to come back. Anyone call?

BUDDY. (*He's still dancing.*) Yeah—a Mr. Copeland— and a Mr. Sampler—cha-cha-cha—

ALAN. (*Looks at him.*) What'd they say?

BUDDY. Nice and easy, cha-cha-cha—

ALAN. (*Angry.*) Hey, Pupi, I'm talking to you.

BUDDY. (*He stops* C.) What's wrong?

ALAN. (*Crosses* L. *to him.*) I'd like to hear one sentence without the rhythm in it. What'd they say?

BUDDY. Who?

ALAN. (*Crossing to him.*) Copeland and Sampler cha-cha-cha!

BUDDY. Nothing. They'll call back later. What's eating you, Alan? (*Pats* ALAN's *shoulder and puts coat on sofa and sits, feet on table.*)

ALAN. It's just a little annoying to have to wait until the dance is over to get my messages. (*He takes coat off sofa, brushes it and hangs it in closet.*)

BUDDY. Boy, you're jumpy lately. You've got a case of nerves, old boy.

ALAN. (*Crossing* D. *to* R. C. *chair.*) Thank you, Docᴛor; is my hour up?

BUDDY. What do you do all day, anyway? You're gone from ten to six. You come home bushed. You keep getting strange calls all day. What's all the mystery?

ALAN. There's no mystery.

BUDDY. (*Feet down; accusingly.*) Have you got a job?

ALAN. No, I haven't got a job. Are you sure no one else called?

BUDDY. You mean Connie?

ALAN. (*A step* L.; *expectantly.*) Connie? Why? Did she—?

BUDDY. No, but you talk about her in your sleep

ALAN. (*Sits* R. C. *chair.*) Me? You're crazy.

BUDDY. Last night you even walked in your sleep. You stretched out your arms and said, "Oh, Connie, darling." —I'm going to have to start locking my door.

ALAN. Are you ribbing me?

BUDDY. Why don't you call her, Alan?

ALAN. What for? I'm not interested. Besides—she checked out of her hotel.

BUDDY. Oh! Where'd she go?

ALAN. How should I know? I didn't ask them.

BUDDY. Maybe she left a forwarding address.

ALAN. There's no forwarding address.

BUDDY. How do you know?

ALAN. I asked them— Look, will you forget about Connie.

BUDDY. Subject closed. (*He rises and crosses* L. *to bar.*) How about a drink?

ALAN. I don't want a drink. (BUDDY *pours one.* ALAN *looks at him.*) What are *you* drinking for?

BUDDY. I like one at night now. Helps me unwind. (*Crossing* R. *of* C. *He drinks.*)

ALAN. What do *you* have to unwind from?

BUDDY. Oh, the little everyday problems of life.

ALAN. (*Rises, crosses* L. *to him.*) Problems? You never had it so good. You sleep till twelve o'clock. Lounge around until two. You go out every night. How do you fill up the rest of the day?

BUDDY. Well, that's one of the little problems I have to unwind from. (ALAN *turns away* R. *disgustedly.*) I'm just having a little fun. What's wrong, Alan?

ALAN. (*Changing his attitude. Turns Upstage, around* R. C. *chair.*) Nothing. Nothing, I'm sorry, kid. I don't know what's wrong with me lately. Listen, I don't feel like sitting in again tonight. You want to go to a movie? Just the two of us? (*Crosses* L. *of chair.*)

BUDDY. (*Puts glass on sofa table.*) Oh, gee, I'd like to, Alan, but I've got a date.

ALAN. Again? That's four times this week. Who's on tonight?

BUDDY. This one's a dancer. Modern jazz. Her name is Snow. (*Step* R.)

ALAN. Snow?

BUDDY. (*Crosses to* ALAN.) Snow Eskanazi!

ALAN. Sounds like an Italian Eskimo.

BUDDY. She's a real weirdo. Wears that white flour on her face like the Japanese Kabuki dancers. But I've got a hunch underneath she's very pretty.

ALAN. Take her out in a strong wind, maybe you'll find out. Where do you collect these girls, anyway? (*Sits* R. C. *chair.*)

BUDDY. I met Snow at that party I went to in the village last Saturday.

ALAN. The one you took the Greek interpreter to?

BUDDY. Yeah. Snow was with an Indian exchange student. I was sitting on the floor next to her and she leans over and gives me her phone number. Just like that.

ALAN. How did Sabu feel about all this?

BUDDY. He loaned her the pencil. Besides, he made a date with the Greek interpreter.

ALAN. (*Sits* R. C. *chair.*) No wonder they have emergency sessions at the U.N.

BUDDY. Like a jerk I went and left early. You know what I hear they played at three o'clock in the morning?

ALAN. What?

BUDDY. Strip Scrabble!

ALAN. Strip Scrabble? I suddenly feel eighty years old. Are you sure you're the same boy who was eating milk and cake over a sink three weeks ago?

BUDDY. (*Crosses* L. *to sofa.*) How about that? What's happened to me, Alan? You've given me a new lease on life. Three weeks here with no one telling me what to do and when to come home. (*Turns to him.*) Well, I'm a different person, aren't I?

ALAN. Different? You're going to need identification before I let you in here again.

BUDDY. That's why I hate to see you moping around like this. (*Crosses* R. *to him.*) You're a different person too. It's not like you to let yourself go. (*Pats his knee.*)

ALAN. (*Jerks knee away; indignantly.*) What do you mean?

BUDDY. Well, you've been sitting home every night, you haven't called a girl in three weeks, you're even getting to look seedy. Why don't you call Rocco tomorrow? (*Crosses away* L. *a step.*)

ALAN. Rocco?

BUDDY. My barber.

ALAN. (*Rises and crosses* L. *to him.*) *Your* barber? What do you mean, *your* barber? *I* sent you there. He's *my* barber.

BUDDY. I know. It was just a figure of speech. I didn't mean anything. You can have him back. (*Fixes* ALAN's *tie.*)

ALAN. I don't want him back. I just want it clear that you only go there. But Rocco is *my* barber. (*Turns away* R., *unfixes his tie.*)

BUDDY. Sure, Alan, sure—

ALAN. (*Mimics.*) Sure, Alan—

BUDDY. Anyway, cheer up. (*He pats* ALAN's *shoulder patronizingly.*) Things'll get better. (ALAN *sits* R. C. *chair. The DOORBELL rings.*) That can't be Snow. It's too early. (*He hops over to door and opens it. It's* PEGGY *in another crazy outfit.*) Oh, hello.

PEGGY. Hello, Mr. Manheim.

BUDDY. (L. *of her.*) Come on in. You know Alan Baker. (*He closes door. He no longer fears the masquerade.*)

PEGGY. (*On foyer.*) Oh, sure. Hi! (*Waves.* ALAN *waves half-heartedly.*) I heard you were back. Is everything all right in Hollywood?

BUDDY. Oh, great. We're just about ready to roll on the picture.

PEGGY. I never got a call. I guess you found someone else for my part.

BUDDY. Not at all. We just have the male lead set. We're still looking for the girl.

PEGGY. Oh? Who did you get?

BUDDY. For what?

PEGGY. The male lead.

BUDDY. Oh. Someone new. An Italian actor.

ALAN. (*Front.*) Rocco La Barber.

PEGGY. Oh, sure. I've heard of him.

BUDDY. Well—if you'll excuse me, I've got to get dressed. I've got to look over some locations tonight.

PEGGY. Of course.

BUDDY. I'll call you. I'm still very interested. (*Shoots his cuff and looks at his watch.*) Great scott, it's nearly seven. (*Smiles at* ALAN *and prances into the bedroom* U. L.)

PEGGY. So young and so brilliant!

ALAN. (*Front.*) Eight colleges are after his brain.

PEGGY. (*Crosses above* ALAN, U. R. *of him.*) I can understand why *he* hasn't called. What's your excuse?

ALAN. (*Rises and starts* L. *to* L. *of* C.) No excuse. I've just been busy.

PEGGY. (*Stepping* D. S.) And I've been lonely, Alan— really lonely.

ALAN. I haven't been doing much either.

PEGGY. (*Crosses* L. *to him.*) You haven't called in nearly three weeks. You never answered my messages.

ALAN. I'm sorry.

PEGGY. (*Swings him around.*) Prove it. Let's go to Connecticut this week end.

ALAN. What's in Connecticut?

PEGGY. (*Putting arm around him.*) The ski lodge.

ALAN. It's Vermont.

PEGGY. I don't care. As long as we're together. How about it?

ALAN. (*Breaking* L.) Well, Peggy—I'm not working any more. I don't have much time for skiing.

PEGGY. (*Angry. Crosses* U. R. *of him.*) You don't have time for anything.

ALAN. (*Crosses* U. L. *of her; stops her.*) Peggy, wait. It's nothing personal. I'm still crazy about you. All right. We'll go this week end.

PEGGY. That's more like my Alan. (*She puts his arms around her.*) Bite me on the neck.

ALAN. What?

PEGGY. Bite me on the neck like you used to.

ALAN. Well, Peggy, I don't really feel—

PEGGY. Oh, come on. (ALAN *shrugs and bites her.*) Ow! You bit me. (*She breaks up to foyer, turns.*) You really

68

must be a vampire. (*She opens door and exits, closing door. ALAN crosses back down to sofa and sits. BUDDY returns wearing a sport jacket. It's one of those multicolored jobs that they advertise every Sunday in the* Times *but no one ever really buys.*)

BUDDY. (*Crosses* D. R. *of* R. C. *chair. He turns around modeling it.*) Well? How do you like the jacket?

ALAN. (*A take.*) I like the lining. What's the jacket like?

BUDDY. How do you think this will go at Sardi's?

ALAN. What are you doing going to Sardi's?

BUDDY. I thought I'd make an impression on Snow. Hey, that reminds me. I'd better make a reservation. (*He crosses* L. *past* ALAN, *picks up phone and dials.*)

ALAN. (*Exaggeratedly swings legs on sofa out of* BUDDY's *way.*) You certainly have blossomed into the Young Man about Town. The theater, the latest styles, Sardi's. I've created an Ivy League Frankenstein.

BUDDY. (*Into phone.*) Hello? I'd like to reserve a table for two for tonight, please. Seven thirty— Oh, you are? (*He covers phone with his hand.*) He says they're all booked up. (*He snaps his fingers, back into phone.*) Are you sure you don't have a reservation for me? Manheim? I'm with M.G.M. (ALAN *throws up his hands. Into phone.*) Yes, it was probably an oversight— Would you? I'd appreciate that— Thanks, so much. Good-bye! (*Hangs up.*) Voila!

ALAN. (*Looks up to heaven.*) *What have I done?*

BUDDY. (*Starts* U. L. *and stops.*) You think he believed me?

ALAN. Why not? *I* did.

BUDDY. I'd better get moving. (*Starts* R. *for foyer and stops and comes* D. R. *of* ALAN.) Oh, by the way, Alan. What are you doing about eleven-thirty tonight?

ALAN. I'll be sitting in a shawl reading the bible. Why?

BUDDY. I hear there's a great picture at the Paris. Why don't you catch the last show? I think it lets out about one.

ALAN. I don't want to be let out about one.

BUDDY. (*Knowingly.*) Well, you see, I thought later on I might drop back here with Snow—for a nightcap.

69

ALAN. You what?

BUDDY. I hate to ask you, Alan, but this may be my night to conquer Mount Everest. You don't mind going to a movie, do you?

ALAN. (*Rises. Seething.*) You're damned right I mind!

BUDDY. What's wrong, Alan? That was our arrangement, wasn't it? If one fellow had a girl—

ALAN. That was *my* arrangement. I did the arranging and *you* went to the movies. Where do you get this *our* stuff?

BUDDY. (*Quite innocently.*) I thought we were splitting everything fifty-fifty?

ALAN. We were, until you got all the fifties. (*Crosses R. of him and turns.*) Boy, what nerve! We're not splitting anything any more. Is that understood? (*Turns.*)

BUDDY. Sure, Alan.

ALAN. (*Turns to him.*) Except the rent. From now on your rent is a hundred forty-two dollars a mouth.

BUDDY. Okay.

ALAN. (*Crosses R. to counter.*) I think I've been big-hearted long enough.

BUDDY. Alan, I never—

ALAN. And buy your own food too. I'm sick and tired of bringing home cookies and watching you finish them reading *my* magazines and watching *my* television.

BUDDY. You're kidding!

ALAN. (*Picks up box and shakes it at him.*) The hell I am! Just keep away from my Fig Newtons!

BUDDY. (*Half chuckles at the ridiculousness of the situation.*) I don't understand. I always give you some of my Yankee Doodles.

ALAN. (*But he's not kidding. Crossing L. to him.*) And stop eating them all over the rug with your crumbs. I never saw anything like it. Clothes lying all over the place. It's disgusting.

BUDDY. Alan, what's eating you? Is it because of this girl?

ALAN. (*Crossing U. L. of sofa.*) Connie? She's got nothing to do with this.

BUDDY. (*Sits sofa, R. end.*) Well, something's bothering you. I'd like to know what.

70

ALAN. Oh, you would, heh? Well, there's plenty bothering me. I happen to think you're pretty ungrateful.

BUDDY. Ungrateful!

ALAN. (*Crossing* R. *of* BUDDY *behind sofa.*) Yes, ungrateful. I took you in here, taught you how to dress and walk and talk. Now look at you. You're a big man.

BUDDY. What's wrong, Alan? You said yourself I should grow up and become a man.

ALAN. I said become *a* man. (*Points to himself.*) Not this man. Don't take my place in life.

BUDDY. How have I taken your place?

ALAN. I run the water for a bath and five minutes later I hear you splashing in there. You're using my barber, my restaurants, my ticket broker, my apartment. How's it going, kid, am I having fun?

BUDDY. You're the one who suggested I do all these things. You said I should start having some fun.

ALAN. I said fun. Have a good time. I didn't say anything about carrying on like this. (*Crosses* R. *of* C.)

BUDDY. Like what?

ALAN. (*Turns.*) Like a bum!

BUDDY. (*Jumps up and Downstage a step.*) A *bum?*

ALAN. You heard me. What kind of crowd are you running around with? (*Crosses to him.*) Intellectual delinquents— Strip Scrabble! You're lucky Interpol didn't rush in there and raid the joint.

BUDDY. What kind of girls do you know? When did that kook upstairs get out of the Girl Scouts?

ALAN. I'm talking to *you!* Where were you until four o'clock the other morning?

BUDDY. What's the difference?

ALAN. (*Crosses and sits* R. C. *chair.*) I want to know where you were until four o'clock in the morning?

BUDDY. Cockle-doodle-doo! What's with you?

ALAN. (*Jumps up.*) Don't cockle-doodle-doo me.

BUDDY. When did you suddenly switch sides? (*Crosses to him.*) When I moved in here you were carrying on like every night was New Year's Eve.

ALAN. We're not talking about a thirty-three-year-old bum. We're talking about a twenty-one-year-old bum.

BUDDY. Oh, you mean it's all right for you.

71

ALAN. I mean, it's not all right for you. (*Crosses* L. *to coffee table.*) Three weeks ago you came in here heartsick over the fate of the world. When was the last time you picked up a newspaper or a book without a phone number in it? What happened to our young hope for a brave new world? (*Turns.*) We're losing half of South America and you're doing the cha-cha.

BUDDY. What's dancing got to do with it?

ALAN. (*Crosses to him.*) And what about looking for a job?

BUDDY. I have been.

ALAN. Since when is the employment office in an espresso joint in the village? You're nothing but a clean-shaven beatnik.

BUDDY. I haven't asked you for anything.

ALAN. You'd have starved to death if Mom hadn't been smuggling pot roast sandwiches through the enemy lines.

BUDDY. I didn't notice you throwing yours in the garbage can.

ALAN. (*Nose to nose.*) At least I call her now and then. You're too busy to worry about her. And have you thought once of how Dad is getting along with the business without either of us there now?

BUDDY. What brought all this on?

ALAN. I'm seeing you for the first time.

BUDDY. You mean you're seeing yourself for the first time. I'm just a carbon copy of you.

ALAN. Well, whoever it is, I don't like it.

BUDDY. Why do *I* get the blame? You go around committing murder and I get the chair.

ALAN. (*He raises his arm threateningly.*) Don't get smart with me. You're not too big yet to get a good slap across the face.

BUDDY. Holy Mackerel, I got two fathers!

ALAN. Cut that out. I'm nothing like him. Nothing at all. (*Turns away* L.)

BUDDY. Well, you certainly don't sound like yourself.

ALAN. (*Turns to him.*) How can I? *You're* myself now.

BUDDY. Well, maybe there's one too many of you around here.

ALAN. Maybe there is. Which one of me is leaving?

BUDDY. It's your apartment. In the meantime, I've got to shave. (*Crosses to bedroom door and* ALAN *crosses* D. C. BUDDY *stops and turns.*) By the way, which is my water, the hot or the cold? (*He stalks out of the room.*)

ALAN. (*At* R. C. *chair.*) How do you like the nerve of that kid? Well, we'll see how big an operator he is without me to supply him with everything. (*Crosses* L. *to bar and pours himself a drink. Tips glass to his mouth and realizes there's nothing in it. He picks up bottle and sees it's empty.*) A whole bottle of Scotch! (*He takes empty bottle, crosses* R. *angrily to bedroom door, waves empty bottle and shouts.*) Bum! (*He starts to bar and the DOORBELL rings. Puts bottle on sofa table.*) Ah, that must be Nanook of the North! This I've got to see. (*He crosses to door and opens it. The* MOTHER *stands there with a heavy valise.*) Mom! Mom, what are you doing here?

MOTHER. (*She trudges into the room, crosses* D. R. C.) I'm lucky I'm here at all. Six blocks I had to lug this from the subway. You'd think a stranger would help a woman. (*She puts down valise and flops in a chair* R. C.)

ALAN. (*Follows* L. *of her.*) Mom, what are you doing with a suitcase? Where are you going?

MOTHER. I'm not going any more. I'm here.

ALAN. Here? Why?

MOTHER. For the same reason Buddy's here— I've run away from home.

ALAN. (*Bends.*) Mom, you're not serious?

MOTHER. Don't think I'm not ashamed. A woman of my age running away from home. I was so humiliated. A woman from my building saw me in the subway with the suitcase. I had to lie to her. I said I was going to visit my brother in California. Then at 125th Street I had to change for a local to come here. She's not so dumb. For California you don't change at 125th Street. I should worry. My life is over anyway.

ALAN. Why, Mom? What happened?

MOTHER. What happened? Ask America what happened! In Alaska they must have heard how that man

73

has been carrying on with me. For three weeks now. Three weeks.

ALAN. All right, Mom, he's very upset. But he'll get over it. He always does.

MOTHER. No, not this time. This time it's different. There's no making up now. I thought maybe there was a chance this morning. I was going to show him I could be bigger than he was. I wanted to show him *I* didn't forget.

ALAN. Forget what?

MOTHER. Today. It's our 37th anniversary.

ALAN. (*Kneels* L. *of her.*) Oh, that's right. Happy anniversary, Mom. (*He kisses her.*)

MOTHER. Thank you, darling. Anyway, I went over to him. I swear to you, I had a big smile on my face, like this: (*She gives a big smile. Then goes back to her sorrow.*) And then as nice as I could possibly say it, I said, "Happy anniversary, darling. I wish you all the happiness in the world." (*She sobs.*) And what do you think he said to me?

ALAN. What?

MOTHER. "Thank you—and I wish you what you wish me." (*She sobs.*) For what? What did I do he should say such a thing?

ALAN. But how do you know he meant anything wrong by that?

MOTHER. Because he knows what I was wishing him. (*She cries.*)

ALAN. (*Throws up his hands in futility. Crossing* U. R. *of her.*) Oh, boy!

MOTHER. All because of you two. He keeps blaming me. "Your bums. Your two bums!"

BUDDY. (*He comes out of the bedroom. Crosses to* L. *of* MOTHER; *leaves jacket on desk.*) Mom? What are you doing here?

MOTHER. (*Crosses* L. *to* BUDDY. *She starts right in on him.*) I'm lucky I'm here at all. Six blocks I had to lug this from the subway.

BUDDY. Whose suitcase is that?

ALAN. My new roommate's! Mom, will you listen to

me? You're just being emotional. You know you can't live here.

BUDDY. Here?

MOTHER. Where else have I got to go? A hotel? Maybe I should move in with his sister Gussie? I'll join the Army first.

ALAN. Mom, it's not that I don't want you. But you wouldn't be comfortable here. It's a small bachelor apartment.

MOTHER. So what am I now? I'm a bachelor too. (*She feels terribly sorry for herself.*) A bachelor with two grown sons.

(*The DOORBELL rings.*)

BUDDY. (*Runs up to door.*) Oh, that's probably Snow.

MOTHER. You're expecting company? (*She picks up suitcase and starts* L. *to bedroom.*) I won't be in your way. I'll go in the bedroom with my sewing.

ALAN. Mom, you don't have to do that.

MOTHER. (*Turns.*) You wouldn't hear me. I'll be like a dead person. (*Continues to bedroom.*)

ALAN. Mom, you don't need your suitcase.

MOTHER. (*Stops at bedroom door and turns.*) It's all right. I want to unpack my Alka Seltzer. Oh, I'm so nauseous. (*She holds her stomach and goes into the bedroom.*)

(*The DOORBELL rings again twice.*)

ALAN. (*Crossing to counter* R. *To* BUDDY.) Well, answer it, lover.

(BUDDY *crosses to door quickly and opens it. The* FATHER *stands there, steaming.*)

BUDDY. Dad!

FATHER. (*He storms in on foyer. To* BUDDY. Where is she? I know she's here. (*To* ALAN.) Where's their mother?

ALAN. (*Weakly.*) In the bedroom.

75

(BUDDY *drifts to* R. *end of sofa.*)

FATHER. Oh, they're hiding them in the bedroom now. What's the matter, the kitchen's being painted? (*He crosses to bedroom and opens door. He looks in.*) Very nice. Very nice for a mother. (BUDDY *crosses and sits on sofa arm* R.)

MOTHER. (*From Offstage.*) What do you want?

FATHER. What is she doing in there?

MOTHER. (*Offstage.*) She's drinking Alka-Seltzer.

FATHER. (*Crossing* D. *below coffee table. Turns away.*) I thought I'd find her in here.

MOTHER. (*She comes out with a glass in her hand. Crossing* D. C.) Where else should I be? They're still my children.

FATHER. She should be home. I'm still her husband.

MOTHER. Not when you treat your own children the way you do.

FATHER. This is something I will not discuss in front of strangers.

MOTHER. They're your sons.

FATHER. They're *your* sons! They're my strangers! (*Crossing* R. C.) Is she coming home?

MOTHER. She's home. This is where she lives now.

FATHER. This is where she lives? With bums?

MOTHER. That's right. So that makes me a bum too. All right? Now you're happy? Now you've got three bums.

ALAN. (*Rises.*) Dad, can I say something?

FATHER. (*Front.*) Who's he talking to? I'm not even here.

BUDDY. (*Crossing* D. L. *of* FATHER.) Can *I* say something?

FATHER. Write it in a play. I'll be there opening night.

(BUDDY *drifts* U. L. *of* R. C. *chair.*)

ALAN. (*Crosses to* FATHER.) All right, Dad, please calm down. Will you talk to me for one minute?

FATHER. (*Crossing* L. *below coffee table.*) Is she coming?

ALAN. Dad, please. It's important.

FATHER. Did the woman hear what I said?

ALAN. All right, don't answer me directly. If you understand, blink your eyes once for "yes" and twice for "no."

FATHER. (*To* MOTHER.) Did she listen to that? If I were here, I'd slap him in the mouth. Is she coming?

BUDDY. Dad, we can't go on like this forever.

FATHER. Forever is over. They'll have no more parents to bother them. They should be very happy.

ALAN. (*Crosses* L. *a step.*) What do you mean, no more parents?

FATHER. (*To* MOTHER.) Tell him. Four months we'll be gone. I've got the tickets in my pocket.

MOTHER. (*Turns.*) You bought the tickets? I told you, I'm not going. Not until everything is all right with you and the boys.

ALAN. Going where?

FATHER. Around the world. (*Crosses* R. C.) Tell him around the world we're going. Ask him if that's far enough?

MOTHER. I'm not going around any worlds.

FATHER. She's going. I've got the tickets in my pocket.

ALAN. Do you mean it? Are you really going?

FATHER. (*Takes ticket out of pocket and holds it up.*) Here! In three weeks we'll be in China. They'll be here bumming around in peace, and we'll be in China—in the middle of a revolution. They'll worry a lot.

ALAN. (*A step to* FATHER.) But how can you leave for four months? Who's going to take care of the business?

FATHER. What business? Tell him? Is she coming around the world—(*Crossing* L. *below coffee table.*) or do I take my sister Gussie?

MOTHER. I told you, I'm not going pleasure cruising with aggravation still on my heart.

ALAN. (*Crosses* L. *to* C.) Dad, what about the business?

FATHER. Is she coming?

MOTHER. Answer him!

FATHER. I answered him. Tomorrow there'll be no business. I'm selling the business. Is that an answer?

ALAN. Selling the business?

BUDDY. Are you serious?

FATHER. Look who's suddenly so shocked. The skier and the Pulitzer Prize winner.

ALAN. (*Crossing* L. *to coffee table.*) Why are you selling it?

FATHER. Who should I save it for, his children?

BUDDY. But who did you sell it to, Dad?

FATHER. Who? To Chiang Kai-shek. (*Crosses* R. *to counter.*) That's why I'm going to China.

ALAN. (*Following* R.) Why, Dad? Are you selling because of us?

FATHER. You? You think I need you two? I did bigger business in the three weeks you were gone than in the six years you were there.

(*The DOORBELL rings.*)

BUDDY. Oh, boy!

FATHER. (*To* MOTHER.) I'm not waiting any more. If she wants, I'll meet her in Hong Kong.

ALAN. Dad, wait. I've got to talk to you about this.

(*DOORBELL rings.*)

BUDDY. (*Looking anxiously to door.*) Can't you talk later?

(*The DOORBELL rings again.*)

MOTHER. Buddy, the doorbell.

BUDDY. (*Crosses* D. R. *to* ALAN.) Alan, what'll I do?

ALAN. Will you take that girl and get out of here? (BUDDY *starts* U. C.)

FATHER. (*Crossing to* BUDDY.) Girl? What girl??

BUDDY. (*Turns.*) Just a girl, Dad. Do you think you could finish this conversation in the bedroom?

FATHER. (*He can't take any more.*) The bedroom? I'll break every bone in his body. (*He raises his arm to hit* BUDDY.)

MOTHER. (*Crossing* D. L.) Harry!

FATHER. (*Follows imitating.*) Harry, Harry.

BUDDY. (*Backing away, crosses to* R. *end sofa.*) Dad, wait—

(*Suddenly the door opens and* CONNIE *enters.*)

CONNIE. (*In foyer.*) Oh, hello!

ALAN. (*Crosses* U. *to* R. *of* CONNIE. *Stunned.*) Connie!

MOTHER. Harry, please, don't say anything.

FATHER. Don't *say* anything? No, I'll sit here and applaud.

ALAN. Connie, where have you been?

CONNIE. Cincinnati.

ALAN. Cincinnati?

CONNIE. (*Crossing* D. R. *to counter.*) With the Electrical Appliance Dealers of America. (ALAN *follows her.*)

FATHER. I don't have to listen to this kind of talk. (*He starts for door* R. *above sofa.* BUDDY *crosses* U. C., *stops him.*)

BUDDY. Dad, wait a minute, please.

ALAN. You mean you did another Industrial Show?

CONNIE. I was Miss Automatic Toaster. I popped up and sang— And after the show three salesmen tried to butter me.

ALAN. But why did you take the job? You said you were quitting.

CONNIE. You changed my mind for me. Look, Alan, this doesn't seem to be the time to discuss this—

ALAN. (*Turns* L. *and back.*) No, no. This is only my mother and father.

FATHER. *Only?*

CONNIE. (*Looks at* MOTHER.) Oh, hello.

MOTHER. (*Sweetly.*) How do you do?

FATHER. (*Crossing* L. *to* R. *of her below sofa. To* MOTHER, *mimicking.*) Are you crazy? "How do you do?"!

ALAN. What do you mean, I changed your mind?

CONNIE. You were right, Alan. I'm much too talented to quit. Besides, I'm beginning to enjoy my work.

ALAN. What work?

FATHER. What do you think, what work? (*To* MOTHER.) You're going to stay here while this is going on?

BUDDY. (*Takes his arm.*) Dad, you don't know what you're saying.

FATHER. (*Lifts arm from shoulder exaggerating movement.*) Pushing? A father you're pushing?

MOTHER. (*Starts up behind sofa table.*) Harry, come in the bedroom.

CONNIE. (*Moves as if to go.*) Alan, call me later.

ALAN. (*Stops her.*) No, tell me what you're talking about.

CONNIE. Well, I really came to say good-bye.

ALAN. Good-bye?

CONNIE. The Electrical Dealers want me to go to Europe. With all expenses paid.

FATHER. (*Shrugs, slaps his thigh. Crosses R. to coffee table.*) She's not ashamed to say it.

CONNIE. It's a wonderful opportunity, Alan. And after all, it's about time I had a "fling."

ALAN. A *fling?*

CONNIE. You know how it is with a twenty-four-year-old girl. She's really not ready to settle down yet.

ALAN. Connie, listen to me.

(The PHONE rings.)

FATHER. (*Points to phone. To* MOTHER.) You hear? That's the cook. She'll be coming to work soon.

(PHONE rings.)

CONNIE. I don't leave until Thursday. Call me, Alan.

BUDDY. (*Crosses R., grabs* FATHER'S *arm.*) Dad, please come inside and talk to me.

FATHER. Again he's pushing.

(BUDDY lets arm go. The PHONE keeps ringing.)

ALAN. Connie, you can't go to Europe. I won't let you.

(PHONE rings.)

MOTHER. Alan, your phone.

CONNIE. You won't *let* me?

ALAN. Connie, I need you. (*PHONE rings.*) I didn't realize it until you were out of my life for three weeks. I couldn't stand it. (*PHONE rings.*) I love you, sweetheart.

MOTHER. (*Crosses to* R. *of* C.) Alan, your phone.

CONNIE. Alan, we've been through those words before.

ALAN. I didn't really feel this way before. (*PHONE rings.*) You've got to believe me. It's all over. I have flung! (*PHONE rings.*)

MOTHER. (*Crosses* L. *to coffee table.*) Buddy, the phone.

BUDDY. Dad—

FATHER. (*To* BUDDY.) If he pushes me once more, he'll bleed from the nose.

BUDDY. I wasn't pushing you.

(*The PHONE rings.*)

MOTHER. Maybe I'm crazy. No one hears a phone (*She picks it up.*)

CONNIE. Alan, are you sure?

MOTHER. (*Into phone.*) Hello?

CONNIE. Are you really sure?

ALAN. I was never so sure of anything in my life.

MOTHER. Alan, it's for you.

ALAN. I'm busy, Mom. Take a message.

MOTHER. Again with a message.

BUDDY. Who is it, Mom?

MOTHER. Do I know? Do I have a pencil?

BUDDY. All right, don't get excited.

FATHER. That's right. Yell at your mother. Push *her!*

BUDDY. I wasn't pushing! (*Crosses above sofa table.*)

MOTHER. Alan, it's a Mr. Kaplon or Koplon— Oh, I'm so nauseous.

FATHER. Copeland? From Begley's Department Store in Texas? Give me that. (*He grabs phone.*)

ALAN. (*Crossing* L.) No, Dad—

(MOTHER *drifts to* R. *of* C., *eyeing* CONNIE *in a friendly way.* CONNIE *steps to* R. *of* R. C. *chair.*)

FATHER. (*Into phone.*) Hello?— Mr. Copeland of Texas?— How do you do, sir?— To what do I owe the honor of this phone call?— Order? What order?— Yes, of course it's Mr. Baker— No, his father— Oh— Just a minute. (*He is bewildered. He looks front but hands* ALAN *phone.*) It's for him.

ALAN. (*Into phone.*) Hello, Mr. Copeland— You what? —Oh, wonderful— The same order we talked about today?— Yes, I've got it. You'll have the shipment the first of the month— Not at all— Have a nice trip back— and thank you— Good-bye. (*He hangs up.*)

FATHER. (*Stares at him.*) How does he come to know Copeland of Texas?

ALAN. I heard he was in town. I called him and took him out to lunch a few times—alone. (*He takes out paper from his pocket.*) I guess *you'd* better take care of this order, Dad.

FATHER. (*He takes paper and looks at it in disbelief.*) Four years I'm after Copeland of Texas.

BUDDY. (*Crosses* D. R. *of* ALAN.) So that's what you've been doing every day. Working. And all those phone calls from Copeland and Sampler.

FATHER. (*Front.*) Sampler too?— I just got a telegram for a big order tonight. For transparent grapes.

ALAN. I thought I owed you that much, Dad.

FATHER. (*To* ALAN.) Owed me? (*Then crosses* L.) He owes me nothing. I don't need his orders. (*Puts order in pocket.*)

ALAN. (*Crosses* L. *to him.*) Dad, please. Even if you don't want me to work for you, can't we at least be friends?

FATHER. (*Angry. Away from* ALAN.) I don't need a bum for a friend.

ALAN. Why am I a bum?

FATHER. Is he married?

ALAN. Yes!

FATHER. Then he's a bu— (*He stops short and turns to* ALAN.) What?

ALAN. That is—I will be if Connie says yes. (*He crosses* R. *to* CONNIE, *who steps to him* R. *of* R. C. *chair.*) Connie, I'll wake up a judge tonight. I'll get down on both knees. I'll do anything, but please . . . won't you marry me?

CONNIE. Oh, darling. (*They kiss.* CONNIE *nudges him.*)

ALAN. Huh! (*Turns to others.*) Mom, I guess you can call the caterers. This is Connie Dayton. The girl I'm going to marry.

BUDDY. No kidding?

(CONNIE *crosses* L. *to* MOTHER. *They meet* R. C.)

MOTHER. Oh, darling. (*She and* CONNIE *embrace.*)

BUDDY. (*Crosses* R. *to* MOTHER.) Gee, congratulations. (*They all look at* ALAN *who then looks for approval from the* FATHER. *They all turn and look at* FATHER.)

ALAN. Dad— (*The* FATHER *turns away from them, front.*)

MOTHER. Harry, your son is going to get married.

FATHER. No one tells me nothing. All I get is pushed.

ALAN. (*Crosses* L. *to* FATHER.) Dad, I don't know how to say this to you—but—well, you were right about so many things. (FATHER *nods "Huh—huh."*) I was a bum. (FATHER *nods "Huh—huh."*) I guess every boy's got to be a bum even for a little while. I just ran into overtime. (FATHER *nods "Huh—huh."*) There's a lot more I want to say to you, Dad, but not now. Look, why don't we all go out to celebrate. To a night club. (*Crosses to* C.)

FATHER. He hasn't got a job, he's going to night clubs.

MOTHER. Harry, the children want to take us out.

FATHER. Let them save their money for furniture.

ALAN. (*Afraid things are going to start all over again; starts* D. L.) Oh, Dad, can't you just once—

CONNIE. (*Stops him.*) No, Alan, Alan. (*Leaping into the breach. Crosses* L. *to* FATHER.) Mr. Baker is right. It's impossible to talk in night clubs anyway. And tonight I'd like to talk. After all, I suddenly have a new family. (*To* FATHER, *tenderly.*) Please, Mr. Baker—why don't we all have dinner together?

FATHER. (*He turns slowly to see who this girl is. She looks "Nice, very nice." And suddenly he has no more sons. Now he's got a daughter. He smiles. Removes hat*

83

and places it over his heart and bows.) Maybe just a cup of coffee.

ALAN. (*Crosses L. to* CONNIE.) Thanks, Dad.

FATHER. (*To* ALAN, *warning.*) But we come home early. You've got to be at the plant eight o'clock in the morning and I don't want any excuses.

ALAN. Do you mean that? Do you really want me back?

FATHER. (*Front.*) No, I'm going to put the night watchman in charge while I'm in China.

ALAN. (*Laughs, starts Upstage, taking* CONNIE.) Come on, everybody.

CONNIE. (*On way up, stops at* BUDDY.) Good night, Buddy. (*She kisses him and continues to foyer.*)

BUDDY. Good night, Connie.

MOTHER. (*Crosses L. to* BUDDY.) Buddy, darling, you do whatever you want, sweetheart. You're not a baby any more.

BUDDY. Thanks, Mom. (*He kisses her.*)

MOTHER. But be up for dinner Friday night.

BUDDY. I will.

MOTHER. And bring your laundry. (*Crosses to bedroom to get valise and coat.*)

BUDDY. (*As* FATHER *starts* U. R. *toward door.*) Well, Dad, you still haven't said anything. Is it okay to leave home?

FATHER. (*Stops* U. L. C.) No.

BUDDY. Oh, Dad!

FATHER. (*Crosses* D. L. *to* BUDDY.) So what are you asking me? (ALAN *crosses* L. *of* FATHER *behind sofa.*) If I say "no," it's "yes" anyway. There was a time when my "no" was "no," but now you're twenty-one and "no" is "yes." So it's "yes" and forget the "no."

BUDDY. Thanks, Dad.

(FATHER *crosses to foyer.* ALAN *takes valise from* MOTHER, *who has come out of bedroom, and they all start out except* BUDDY, CONNIE *leading,* FATHER *last.*)

ALAN. (*Has put on coat.*) See you back here later? About twelve?

BUDDY. Make it one.

ALAN. (*Smiles.*) Right, Mr. Manheim. (*He goes to the open door and turns.*) So long—bum! (*He exits, closing door.*)

BUDDY. (*He looks after him, crosses to* U. L. *desk and gets jacket. Puts jacket on and looks around room. He crosses now to sofa and arranges pillows. DOORBEL rings. Crosses to* D. L. *lamp and turns it out.*) Coming, snowflake! (*He goes to door, composes himself, opens it. (A* WOMAN *in her fifties stands there.*) Gussie!

(*CURTAIN starts down.*)

WOMAN. (*She walks into room, crosses* D. R. C., *sits* R. C. *chair, as* BUDDY *follows.*) I was in the neighborhood, so I thought I'd say hello.

CURTAIN

PROPERTY PLOT

SET PROPS
Bar stool with back and swivel seat, D. R.
Chair upholstered with arms, D. R. C.
Chair upholstered no arms, R of fireplace
Chair upholstered no arms, L of fireplace
Knee-hole chair, Up L of counter cabinet
Bar table behind sofa, D. L. C.
Sofa upholstered, curved, D. L. C.
Coffee table below sofa, D. L. C.
Large table lamp and shade, On cabinet D. L. of window
Curtain draw type, at window

SET PROPS: *Decor.*

Kitchen:
On counter:
 Aluminum teapot, L.
 Coffee pot, C.
 Three small pots nesting, R.
On wall below cabinet hanging:
 Orange frying pan, L.
Top of cabinet:
 Two green candlesticks, L.

Fireplace:
Standing rack with 3 fireplace tools, U. R. corner
Potted plant on fireplace bench, R end of fireplace
Andirons and birch logs on fireplace bench, C.
Antique pistol on R. wall, R. of fireplace
Wall plaque above pistol, wooden, R of fireplace
Gold key on R. wall, L. of fireplace
Wall plaque above key, wooden, L of fireplace

Foyer:
Chandelier; three branch

Desk Area:
Wall phone on U. L. wall
Gold and white sunburst on U. L. wall, L. of wall phone and above
Black dancer figurine top shelf on U. L. wall
White horse figurine top shelf on L wall
Black Mermaid figurine, 2nd L shelf
2 Black bookends on bottom U. S. shelf
Silver woman on bench figurine on 1st U. S. shelf
Sulky driver an horse figurine on 1st L. shelf

2 Framed automobile prints under 1st U. S. shelf
Art poster on L wall above 2nd shelf
83 Books on 1st and 2nd U. S. and L shelves
White marble figure of woman on L. counter U. S. end of
    window
Large plant in copper holder on L. counter, C.
Plant in square black holder D. L. counter corner, R. of lamp
Black waste paper basket under desk, U. L. C.
Black ceramic ash tray U. S. counter, C.
Brass ash tray on L. counter, below R. of window
2 pillows sofa

SMALL PROPS:
Beige desk—telephone
Magazines—2 doz. assorted (art studies, show & topical)
6 Highball glasses
6 Cocktail glasses
Liquor bottles—(Vermouth, Scotch, Gin, Bourbon & Rum)
Soda—quart size
Gingerale—quart size
Plastic bottle caps
Ice bucket—modern thermal & tongs
Water pitcher—thermal, pint size
Address and number book
Cigarette box
Cigarettes
Cigarette holder
Box of matches—wooden
Table lighter
Cigarette lighter
2 doz. pencils in holder
Writing paper—white 7 x 9
Suitcases—Weekend size, chic, (PEGGY) ; club bag, (ALAN) ;
    black gladstone (BUDDY) ; modern (CONNIE) ; brown,
    (MOTHER)
Packaged bottle of Scotch
Empty box fig newtons
Hat box containing ski hat
Brass ash tray with butts
Brass ash tray clean
Letter to Dad from Buddy
Steamship tickets
Order form
Towel
Alka Seltzer
Wooden tray

ACT ONE

CHECK LIST:

On Set:
Foyer—
Suitcase, (PEGGY) in foyer L. of C. off with Peggy
Suitcase, (ALAN) below Peggy's off with Alan

Fireplace:
Scatter 8 magazines on fireplace bench

U. S. *Desk Area:*
Scatter 8 magazines
Hand towel U. S.
Ice bucket with ice below towel
Wooden tray holding 4 highball glasses & 4 cocktail glasses below ice bucket
8 Assorted liquor bottles against wall above tray with glasses
Packaged bottle Scotch against L wall 3rd bottle up from window, behind glasses
Water pitcher half filled on tray with 2 glasses below R end of window
R end of window open
Curtain open
Plastic caps on soda and gingerale (caps to fit loosely)
Soda and gingerale below liquor bottles
Scatter 4 magazines

Bar Table Behind Sofa:
Scatter 4 magazines, 1 sheet writing paper under a book at L end of bar table

Down Left Counter:
Pencils in holder

Coffee Table:
Ash tray with butts left corner away from sofa
Ash tray clean (place several drops of water in it) to R of filled ash tray
Cigarette box with cigarettes below ash trays, C
Cigarette holder left corner near sofa
Cigarette lighter to R of holder
Wooden matches to R of cigarette lighter
Table lighter to R of matches
Desk phone R. of C.
Address book R of phone

Sofa:
1 pillow R. of C. of sofa
1 pillow L end sofa

Bar Stool facing U. S.

Check Door Knobs
Closet
Trench coat—Alan's
2 Sport jackets
Silk smoking jacket—Buddy's

Bedroom
Sport jacket—Alan's

Prop Table Off U. R.
Suitcase—Buddy's off with Buddy in bedroom
Hat box on with Connie

ACT TWO

CHECK LIST:
Check pencils and paper D. L. counter and bar table

Prop Table Off U. R.
Letter for Dad on with Dad and off with Dad
Suicase—Connie's

ACT THREE

CHECK LIST:

Strike:
Hat box
Empty carton scotch
Pencils (return to D. L. counter)
Glasses from fireplace
Remove 3 liquor bottles from L counter

Rearrange:
Chair R. of fireplace facing D. S. socks on back
Chair L. of fireplace facing U. S., 2 shirts on back
Towel and shirt over L rail
Pr. socks over back of desk chair
Socks on desk
Ice bucket moves down on L. counter at U. S. end of window
Water pitcher to U. S. counter C.
2 dishes on kitchen counter
Close curtain
Bar stool facing D. S.
Coffee table reset as in 1st act

Set:
D. R. counter two glasses of water
Empty fig newton box

Left Counter:
Bottle Scotch with enough for one drink on wooden tray with 5
   glasses

Bar Table:
Book back to U. S. counter

Prop Table:
Suitcase—Mother's
Order form—Alan's
Steamship ticket—Dad's

Off Bedroom:
Glass Alka-Seltzer—Mother's

COSTUMES

ALAN—*Act One*
Green suede & knit sweater
Brown slacks
Mahogany loafers
Light tan & brown ascot
Tan open neck shirt
Brown single breasted jacket (change to)
Trench coat (in closet)

Act Two
Same as end of Act One

Act Three
Light grey glen plaid single breasted suit
White shirt
Black tie
Black shoes
Dark brown ascot
Black socks

BUDDY—*Act One and Two*
Herringbone fly front dark overcoat
Charcoal grey single breasted suit
Black and white thin striped shirt
Blue stripe tie
Black loafers
Blue shantung velvet collar smoking jacket (in closet-change to)

Act Three
Brown-olive slacks
Pink shirt
Brown pattern tie
Pink green, yellow plaid silk sport jacket
(in bedroom-change to)

AUNT GUSSIE—*Act Three*
Royal blue wool dress
Royal blue hat and veil
Royal blue mink trimmed coat
Light blue handbag and white gloves
Pearl necklace and earrings

FATHER—*Act One and Two*
Tan polo coat
Brown hat
Black shoes
White shirt, cuff links
Grey pin stripe flannel suit
Red pattern tie

Act Three
Same polo coat and hat
Black glen plaid single breasted suit
Grey tie
Handkerchief

MOTHER—*Act One and Two*
Green wool dress and pearl pin
Brown suede pumps
Brown leather handbag
Off white gloves
Brown, green and coral feather hat
Brown cloth coat trimmed at neck and wrists with beaver double
    breasted

Act Three
Purple dress with jacket and pearl pin
Stadium boots, brown and tan suede
Purple hat satin
Brown gloves
Double strand pearls
Big button pearl earrings
Grey wig thru out

PEGGY—*Act One*
White nylon fleece silk plaid lined jacket
White nylon fleece hat
Purple white patterned heavy wool sweater
Purple ski pants
Purple ankle length kid boots
Pearl bangle bracelet and earrings
Coral scarf at neck of sweater

Act Two
Coral jersey culottes—lounging pajamas
Dark pink large rhinestone bracelet and earrings
Rose satin strap shoes
Coral wool coat

Act Three
Roman stripe crepe de chine sheath, lime belt with jewel
Lime shantung shoes
2 gold bracelets, multi jeweled and earrings to match

CONNIE—*Act One*
Orange wool jersey dress
Orange bow in hair
Gold chain necklace and gold pin at neck
Pearl and gold chain bracelet
Leopard Eton jacket
Elbow length tan leather gloves
Tan satchel type handbag
Tan shoes

Act Two
Yellow lime wool dress
Black bead necklace and bracelets
Black hair bow
Black lizard shoes
White coat
Black alligator bag

Act Three
Turquoise suit single breasted
White coat
Black shoes
Black bag
Turquoise and pearl necklace, pearl button earrings
Silk blouse

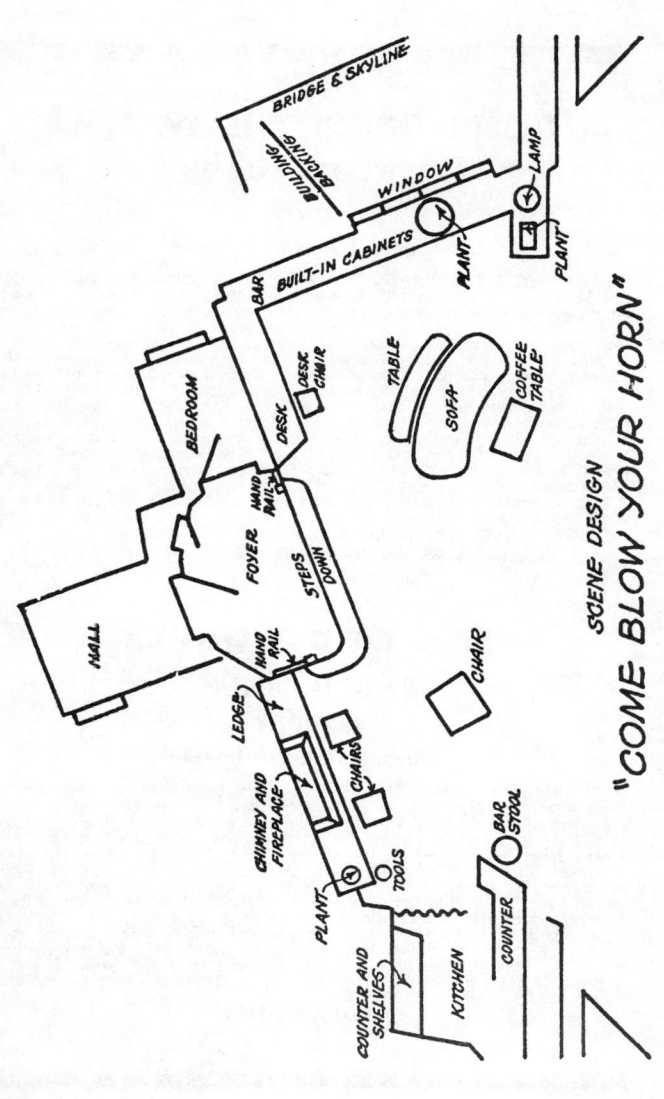

SCENE DESIGN

"COME BLOW YOUR HORN"

DON'T DRINK THE WATER

By WOODY ALLEN

FARCE

12 men, 4 women—Interior

A CASCADE OF COMEDY FROM ONE OF OUR FUNNIEST CO-MEDIANS, and a solid hit on Broadway, this affair takes place inside an American embassy behind the Iron Curtain. An American tourist, ca-terer by trade, and his family of wife and daughter rush into the embassy two steps ahead of the police, who suspect them of spying and picture-taking. But it's not much of a refuge, for the ambassador is absent and his son, now in charge, has been expelled from a dozen countries and the whole continent of Africa. Nevertheless, they carefully and frantically plot their escape, and the ambassador's son and the caterer's daughter even have time to fall in love. "Because Mr. Allen is a working comedian him-self, a number of the lines are perfectly agreeable . . . and there's quite a delectable bit of business laid out by the author and manically elab-orated by the actor. . . . The gag is pleasantly outrageous and impeccably performed."—*N. Y. Times.* "Moved the audience to great laughter. . . . Allen's imagination is daffy, his sense of the ridiculous is keen and gags snap, crackle and pop."—*N. Y. Daily News.* "It's filled with funny lines. . . . A master of bright and hilarious dialogue."—*N. Y. Post.*

(Slightly restricted. Royalty, $50-$25, where available.)

THE ODD COUPLE

By NEIL SIMON

COMEDY

6 men, 2 women—Interior

NEIL SIMON'S THIRD SUCCESS in a row begins with a group of the boys assembled for cards in the apartment of a divorced fellow, and if the mess of the place is any indication, it's no wonder that his wife left him. Late to arrive is another fellow who, they learn, has just been sep-arated from his wife. Since he is very meticulous and tense, they fear he might commit suicide, and so go about locking all the windows. When he arrives, he is scarcely allowed to go to the bathroom alone. As life would have it, the slob bachelor and the meticulous fellow decide to bunk together—with hilarious results. The patterns of their own disastrous mar-riages begin to reappear in this arrangement; and so this too must end. "The richest comedy Simon has written and purest gold for any theatre-goer. . . . This glorious play."—*N. Y. World-Telegram & Sun.* "His skill is not only great but constantly growing. . . . There is scarcely a moment that is not hilarious."—*N. Y. Times.*

(Royalty, $50-$35.)

THE GOOD DOCTOR

NEIL SIMON

(All Groups) Comedy

2 Men, 3 Women. Various settings.

With Christopher Plummer in the role of the Writer, we are introduced to a composite of Neil Simon and Anton Chekhov, from whose short stories Simon adapted the capital vignettes of this collection. Frances Sternhagen played, among other parts, that of a harridan who storms a bank and upbraids the manager for his gout and lack of money. A father takes his son to a house where he will be initiated into the mysteries of sex, only to relent at the last moment, and leave the boy more perplexed than ever. In another sketch a crafty seducer goes to work on a wedded woman, only to realize that the woman has been in command from the first overture. Let us not forget the classic tale of a man who offers to drown himself for three rubles. The stories are droll, the portraits affectionate, the humor infectious, and the fun unending.

"As smoothly polished a piece of work as we're likely to see all season."—*N.Y. Daily News*. "A great deal of warmth and humor —vaudevillian humor—in his retelling of these Chekhovian tales."—*Newhouse Newspapers*. "There is much fun here . . . Mr. Simon's comic fancy is admirable."—*N.Y. Times*.

(Music available. Write for particulars.)
ROYALTY, $50-$35

The Prisoner of Second Avenue

NEIL SIMON

(All Groups) Comedy

2 Men, 4 Women, Interior

Mel is a well-paid executive of a fancy New York company which has suddenly hit the skids and started to pare the payroll. Anxiety doesn't help; Mel, too, gets the ax. His wife takes a job to tide them over, then she too is sacked. As if this weren't enough, Mel is fighting a losing battle with the very environs of life. Polluted air is killing everything that grows on his terrace; the walls of the high-rise apartment are paper-thin, so that the private lives of a pair of German stewardesses next door are open books to him; the apartment is burgled; and his psychiatrist dies with $23,000 of his money. Mel does the only thing left for him to do: he has a nervous breakdown. It is on recovery that we come to esteem him all the more. For Mel and his wife and people like them have the resilience, the grit to survive.

"Now all this, mind you, is presented primarily in humorous terms."—*N.Y. Daily News*. "A gift for taking a grave subject and, without losing sight of its basic seriousness, treating it with hearty but sympathetic humor . . . A talent for writing a wonderfully funny line . . . full of humor and intelligence . . . Fine fun."—*N.Y. Post*. "Creates an atmosphere of casual cataclysm, and everyday urban purgatory of copelessness from which laughter seems to be released like vapor from the city's manholes."—*Time*.

ROYALTY, $50-$35

The Gingerbread Lady

NEIL SIMON
(Little Theatre) Comedy-Drama
3 Men, 3 Women—Interior

Maureen Stapleton played the Broadway part of a popular singer who has gone to pot with booze and sex. We meet her at the end of a ten-week drying out period at a sanitarium, when her friend, her daughter, and an actor try to help her adjust to sobriety. But all three have the opposite effect on her. The friend is so constantly vain she loses her husband; the actor, a homosexual, is also doomed, and indeed loses his part three days before an opening; and the daughter needs more affection than she can spare her mother. Enter also a former lover louse, who ends up giving her a black eye. The birthday party washes out, the gingerbread lady falls off the wagon and careens onward to her own tragic end.

"He has combined an amusing comedy with the atmosphere of great sadness. His characteristic wit and humor are at their brilliant best, and his serious story of lost misfits can often be genuinely and deeply touching."—N.Y. Post. "Contains some of the brightest dialogue Simon has yet composed."—N.Y. Daily News. "Mr. Simon's play is as funny as ever—the customary avalanche of hilarity, and landslide of pure unbuttoned joy . . . Mr. Simon is a funny, funny man—with tears running down his cheek."—N.Y. Times.

Royalty $50-$35

The Sunshine Boys

NEIL SIMON
(All Groups) Comedy
5 Men, 2 Women

An ex-vaudeville team, Al Lewis and Willie Clarke, in spite of playing together for forty-three years, have a natural antipathy for one another. (Willie resents Al's habit of poking a finger in his chest, or perhaps accidentally spitting in his face). It has been eleven years since they have performed together, when along comes CBS-TV, who is preparing a "History of Comedy" special, that will of course include Willie and Al—the "Lewis and Clark" team back together again. In the meantime, Willie has been doing spot commercials, like for Schick (the razor blade shakes) or for Frito-Lay potato chips (he forgets the name), while Al is happily retired. The team gets back together again, only to have Al poke his finger in Willie's chest, and accidentally spit in his face.

". . . the most delightful play Mr. Simon has written for several seasons and proves why he is the ablest current author of stage humor."—Watts, N. Y. Post. "None of Simon's comedies has been more intimately written out of love and a bone-deep affinity with the theatrical scene and temperament." Time. ". . . another hit for Neil Simon in this shrewdly balanced, splendidly performed and rather touching slice of the show-biz life."—Watt, New York Daily News. "(Simon) . . . writes the most dependably crisp and funny dialogue around . . . always well-set and polished to a high lustre."—WABC-TV. ". . . a vaudeville act within a vaudeville act . . . Simon has done it again."—WCBS-TV.

Royalty $50-$35